Stars in Your Bones

For Mark St Pierre —
Blessings on Your own spiritual path.
Julia Barkley

We lovingly dedicate this book to the
explorers and storytellers of the future,
who will continue to tell the cosmic stories
in healing and creative ways.
May they find strength and inspiration
to shape visions of on-going creation
and to give them voice.

Stars in Your Bones

Emerging Signposts on Our Spiritual Journeys

Alla Renée Bozarth
Julia Barkley
Terri Berthiaume Hawthorne

NORTH STAR PRESS OF ST. CLOUD, INC.

Some of the poems in Stars in Your Bones first appeared elsewhere:

"Godmothers of a New Creation," Journal of Women's Ministries, Vol. 5, No. 1, Winter 1989.

"Passover Remembered," The Witness, Vol. 67, No. 7, July 1984.

"Pearls" and "Water Women," WomanSpirit, Vol. 9, No. 36, Summer 1983.

The following poems appear in these books by Alla Renée Bozarth (Alla Bozarth-Campbell):

At the Foot of the Mountain, 1990, CompCare Publishers, Minneapolis, Minnesota: "Family Reunion," "Godmothers of a New Creation," and "Mama Sea and Mama Rock."

Womanpriest, 1988 (revised edition), Luramedia, San Diego, California: "Bakerwoman God," "Call," "Creation," "God Is a Verb," "Gynergy," "Mother Christ/Sister Spirit," "Passover Remembered," "Pearls," "Water Women," "You Need to Know," and "I AM."

Love's Prism, 1987, Sheed and Ward, St. Louis, Missouri: "Gynergy," "Love Mantra for Letting Go," "Sunday Memory," and "Travail."

Life Is Goodbye/Life Is Hello, 1986 (revised edition), CompCare Publishers, Minneapolis, Minnesota: "Eskimo Crone" ("Visiting the Old Folks' Home"), "Love Mantra for Letting Go," and "Loving the Body."

Sparrow Songs, 1982 (with René Bozarth), Wisdom House, Minneapolis, Minnesota: "Braids," "Five Trees," "For Julia," "Has Anyone Ever Died of Bad Dreams?", "Love Mantra for Letting Go," "Mama Sea and Mama Rock," and "Women at Play."

In the Name of the Bee & the Bear & the Butterfly, 1978, Wisdom House, Minneapolis, Minnesota: "Creation," "Crosses," "Gloria," and "God Is a Verb."

Gynergy, 1978, Wisdom House, Minneapolis, Minnesota: "Bakerwoman God," "Call," "Gynergy," "Liberation Song," "Mother Christ/Sister Spirit," "Mother with the Moon in Your Mouth," "Out of the Corner Not Fighting," "Rape Poem," "Sisterhood is Synergy," "Song of Mary," and "Travail."

Terri Hawthorne's Emerging Patterns Web first appeared in in The Goddess in the Age of Quantum Physics, 1988, Tara Publications.

Reclaiming the Goddess is based on material first presented in The Many Faces of the Great Mother, 1987, Tara Publications.

The New Sciences is based on material first presented in The Goddess in the Age of Quantum Physics, 1988, Tara Publications.

Library of Congress Cataloging-in-Publication Data

Bozarth, Alla. 1947-
    Stars in your bones : emerging signposts on our spiritual journeys / Alla Renée Bozarth, Julia Barkley, Terri Berthiaume Hawthorne.
    112 p. 28 cm.
    ISBN: 0-87839-057-X : $19.95
    1. Women--Religious life. 2. Women and religion. I. Barkley, Julia, 1924- . II. Hawthorne, Terri Berthiaume, 1942- . III. Title.
BL625.7B69 1990
291'.082--dc20   90-35127
                                                    CIP

Design: Corinne A. Dwyer
Photography: Terri Berthiaume Hawthorne

ISBN: 0-87839-057-X
Copyright © 1990 Alla Renée Bozarth (poetry), Julia Barkley (paintings), and Terri Berthiaume Hawthorne (text).

Printed and bound in the United States of America by Sentinel Printing Company, Sauk Rapids, Minnesota.

Published by North Star Press of St. Cloud, Inc., P.O. Box 451, St. Cloud, Minnesota, 56302.

Acknowledgments
A special thanks for the contributions of Sr. Judith Stoughton and Jack Hawthorne.

Contents

Introduction

Call

There is a new sound
of roaring voices in the deep
and light shattered rushes in the heavens;
the mountains are coming alive,
the fire-kindled mountains, moving again
to reshape the earth.
It is we sleeping women,
waking up in a darkened world,
cutting the chains from off our bodies
with our teeth, stretching our lives
over the slow earth,
seeing, moving, breathing in the vigor
that commands us to make all things new.

It has been said that while the women sleep,
the earth shall sleep.
But listen! We are waking up and rising,
and soon our sister will know her strength.
The earth-moving day is here.
We women wake to move in fire.
The earth shall be remade.

*This poem was written on the eve of
Alla's ordination to the priesthood—
July 29, 1974.*

   In January 1975, I first read "Call" in a newspaper feature article written
about Alla Bozarth following her irregular Episcopal ordination to the priesthood
with ten other women. At the time I was involved with a group of Roman Catholic
women who were seeking ordination for women into the diaconate. I was very
moved by this poem. It seemed to me to capture what so many of us were feeling.
Women of many denominations were being ordained. Roman Catholic women

were organizing and speaking out in the face of discrimination. Together we were growing in awareness of institutionalized sexism and racism, and we were concerned with ecological and peace issues. We believed, with many of our sisters and brothers, that once we became aware of injustices, we would point them out and all fair-minded people would join us in removing oppression and creating a more equitable and just society. We thought it would be easy. Today we know better.

I was so impressed with Alla's poem that I called her and asked if I could use it in a documentary I was preparing about women and ministry in the Roman Catholic church. When we met, she not only gave me many more poems, but taped several of them for me to use in the documentary, which I named "A New Call."

In the fall of 1975, I had joined an exciting and innovative program at The College of Saint Catherine in St. Paul, Minnesota. It was called the Feminist Art Core, and it was a unique opportunity to do integrated, creative feminist studies in a program designed by Sister Judith Stoughton, Carole Fisher and Sister Ann Jennings. The program was based on the Women's Building in Los Angeles created by Judy Chicago, Arlene Raven, Sheila de Bretville and Ruth Iskin. In this stimulating setting, with thirty other women ranging in age from nineteen to forty-five, I began to explore more deeply women's art and history and to develop my own creativity and skills. In our collective research, we found the Goddess. We celebrated both the Goddesses in history and the Goddess Within each of us.

During this time, Sister Judith introduced me to Julia Barkley. She knew I would appreciate and understand Julia's paintings. Julia had already made contact with Alla. So our paths merged. In the ensuing years we have shared interests, concerns, projects, art and our lives.

Feminist scholarship believes that knowledge is a human construct. This means it is impossible to be totally objective, and it is best to acknowledge one's frame of reference. How we live, our life experiences, our families, friends and colleagues help to shape the way we think, write, make art, do research and affect the conclusions we reach. Julia, Alla and I have different backgrounds, religious affiliations, histories and families. This book is limited by the fact that we are all white, middle class, heterosexual and were raised in Christian traditions. We do not presume to speak for all women in all cultures, or even for all women in our own. We share the insights we have gathered in the hopes that they will prove useful to other journeyers along the way.

In her poem, "Passover Remembered" (1984), written in commemoration of her tradition-breaking ordination to the priesthood, Alla reflects on the decade following that event. The poem speaks of taking risks, moving quickly, of being misunderstood; it speaks of the joys of the journey. It has been translated into Spanish and circulated in the underground Sanctuary movement to hearten those in exile. Like many art works, it forms a symbol, bigger than Alla's individual or even our collective story. I believe it chronicles the journeys of many individual women as well as telling the story of the women's movement during these years. Some shelters and programs for battered women pass this poem out to newcomers to en-courage them. Alla speaks of being "In the open desert where no signposts are. Make maps as you go, remembering the way back from before you were born."

Patterns are emerging—not the "one right way"—but some of the ways/paths/journeys that many women and men are traveling are becoming clearer.

Some of these patterns began to emerge for us when Julia, Alla and I began to collaborate on this book. In reading the titles of Julia's art exhibitions, we realized that all three of us had been exploring the same spiritual paths for the last twenty years. We were finally at a point where we could name some of the landmarks, perhaps making the paths a little easier for those who follow.

We believe that Julia Barkley's exhibition titles form some of the "signposts," and that the paintings, poems and writings presented here can serve as "maps." Artists are often prophets giving "voice" to new ideas in their art work. In reviewing hundreds of Julia's paintings and hundreds of Alla's poems in books and manuscripts, I began to see the exhibition titles and themes as metaphors for women's spiritual journeys of the 1970s and 1980s.

Julia Barkley's Exhibition Titles

The Energy of Miracles: Reclaiming the Stories of Judeo-Christian Tradition
The Great Mother: From Astarte to the Virgin Mary
Circle of Fire: A Requiem for the Estimated Nine Million Women Burned as Witches
Consolation of Souls, Hiroshima: The Death of the Earth Mother
Gaia Celebrations: Landscapes that Portray the Strength and Energy of the Earth
Visions of Native Americans: Explorations of the Indian Theme of Unity with
    Nature
Stars in Your Bones: Portraying the Universe as an Interconnected Whole

Theologian Thomas Berry, in his book *The New Story* (1978), pointed out the cultural and planetary significance of a common creation story. He believed our culture was experiencing a failure of cosmology; our stories of creation were too limiting and too small for what we know of our universe today. Physicist Brian Swimme, in an article entitled "The Cosmic Creation Story," in *The Re-Enchantment of Science* (1988), by David Griffith, said that our society desperately needs to support, encourage and listen to its artists, the storytellers who can convey these new stories.

I created the Emerging Patterns Web as a visual construction of these spiritual journeys. I use a web because, while we can chart our journeys by Julia's exhibition themes, we did not experience them as hierarchal, causal steps. The patterns form an interconnected web; they merge. We can pass back and forth between concepts. Not all of us will spend time in each category, or equal time in each. Some of us will be satisfied to stay in one section; some of us may try two or three. And some of us may swing freely among many. As will be seen, many of the images and ideas presented in this book fit into more than one category.

These patterns form guides, not laws.

Even so, this web provides a framework for discussing feminist theology and practice. There are many different threads and focuses in feminist thought. There is no one body of dogma or set of beliefs. The web titles became the chapters of *Stars in Your Bones* and delineate the form of the book. It could have taken other forms.

Some of us are revisionists, reclaiming the feminine within our own traditions.
Some of us are re-claiming the Goddess, the Goddess Within each woman and the
    Goddesses throughout history.
Some of us are fighting oppressions of sexism, racism, heterosexism, classism,
    colonialism and poverty directly.
Some of us are focusing on the protection of the earth and her children through the
    ecological, peace and holistic health movements.
Some of us are practicing and studying tribal earth-centered traditions.
Some of us are looking to new discoveries in science to form new interpretations
    and philosophies of spirituality.
Many of us are doing various combinations of the web.

Emerging Signposts on Our Spiritual Journeys

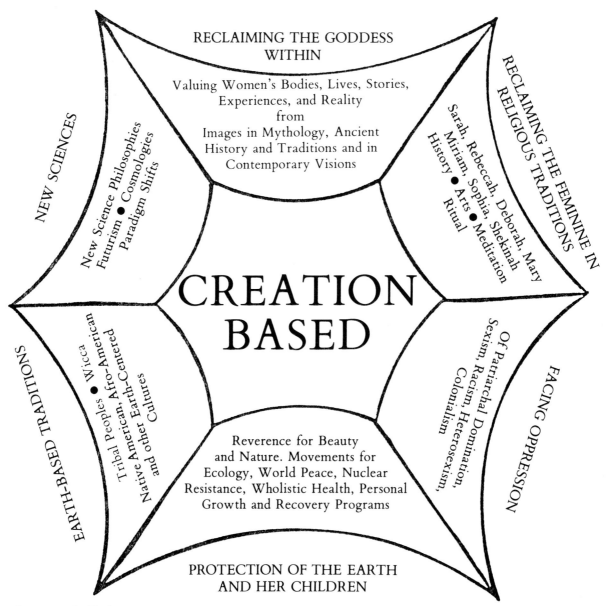

RECLAIMING THE GODDESS WITHIN

Valuing Women's Bodies, Lives, Stories, Experiences, and Reality from Images in Mythology, Ancient History and Traditions and in Contemporary Visions

NEW SCIENCES

New Science Philosophies Futurism ● Cosmologies Paradigm Shifts

RECLAIMING THE FEMININE IN RELIGIOUS TRADITIONS

Sarah, Rebeccah, Deborah, Mary Miriam, Sophia, Shekinah History ● Arts ● Meditation Ritual

CREATION BASED

EARTH-BASED TRADITIONS

Wicca ● Tribal Peoples, Afro-American Native American, Earth-Centered and other Cultures

FACING OPPRESSION

Of Patriarchal Domination, Sexism, Racism, Heterosexism, Colonialism

Reverence for Beauty and Nature. Movements for Ecology, World Peace, Nuclear Resistance, Wholistic Health, Personal Growth and Recovery Programs

PROTECTION OF THE EARTH AND HER CHILDREN

This web was spun by Terri Hawthorne from threads provided by Julia Barkley's art exhibition themes and Alla Bozarth's poems.

It is ironic to me that I am a pattern shaper. As a feminist scholar and counselor, I have often felt frustrated by labeling and categories. I have often found words and language limiting and not fitting my life experiences nor those of other women.

Today, women philosophers and educators are reviewing why it did not work when we tried adding women and minorities and ethnic studies to mainstream curriculum. Just adding new names and stories did not work because these did not fit the dominant categories. So, feminist scholars returned to the Greek classics and foundations of Western thinking. We began to look at when, how and why these categories were formed and shaped. Most of our base values came out of a time period when a small elite group of propertied, often slave-holding men defined themselves as the *inclusive norm* for all of us. Women and most men were deliberately excluded from this norm.

In the foreword to Alice Walker's *Temple of My Familiar*, Lissie Lyles says, "If they lied about me, they have lied about everything."

Feminist scholarship begins with critique. Philosopher Elizabeth Minnich says, "Everything based on excluding the majority is fundamentally wrong. . . . Feminist thought takes nothing as given or settled for all time. It accepts no truth as revealed and holds none to be directly reflective of what is 'natural.'"

This unwillingness to label or lock in the "one right way to believe," the "one truth," is the basis of much feminist theology. It explains our hesitancy in setting forth patterns, our basing our knowledge on life experiences and stories, and our attention to multiplicity, diversity and to art forms.

And yet, patterns have always been a useful tool. Today, new ways of naming are emerging. Sometimes this is evident in the forms themselves—webs, spirals and quilts—sometimes in the combination of academic information with creative modes—art, meditation or ritual. We are attempting to make room for and acknowledge multiple ways of knowing. What is different and emerging are new ways to present the patterns. Special care is paid to establishing a specific viewpoint. Our sisters of color have reminded us that replacing a universal white Western male norm with a universal white Western female norm is not much progress. We agree. In acknowledging our frame of reference as we proceed with engaged scholarship, we hope to point out the fallacies that knowledge can be totally factual and purely objective. It cannot.

Novaya Zemlya

Explorers at earth's
pinnacle below the Pole Star
may, without going mad,
hear directly the growl
of the Great Bear,

see sunrise in a solar mirage
hours before it happens,
encircling the world
in a single hour
they believe to last days.

All inner adventure
begins here.
This is the place
of illusion and
unfinal reality.

No one escapes
the caution:
all things are
fashioned oddly,
the joints of the universe
mysteriously hinged.

Do not, therefore, attempt
to name things too clearly,
or imagine the crystal vision
you see to be precisely itself.

All things are born
and flow again
in realms of the magi.

Our lives—Julia's, Alla's and mine—have touched "at the crossroads" many times. Several years may pass between meetings, and yet, upon sharing work, we find strength in that, synchronistically, our ideas and poems and visions are in tune. Even so, we are not in absolute agreement on all points, and we struggle at times to appreciate our differences. In this collaborative work, we speak in multi-voices to guide and enable the viewer/reader to remember and elucidate her/his own journey.

Blessings to you on your paths.　　　　　　　Terri Berthiaume Hawthorne

Passover Remembered

Ten years so far
in the wilderness,
ten summers and hundreds
of spring storms since
we few ventured out
into the vast heartland.

How quickly it happened,
only a few days' notice
for some of us:

Pack nothing.
Bring only
your determination
to serve and
your willingness
to be free.

Don't wait for the bread to rise.
Take nourishment for the journey,
but eat standing, be ready
to move at a moment's notice.

Do not hesitate to leave
your old ways behind—
fear, silence, submission.

Only surrender to the need
of the time—to love
justice and walk humbly
with your God.

Do not take time
to explain to the neighbors.
Tell only a few trusted
friends and family members.

Then begin quickly,
before you have time
to sink back into
the old slavery.

Set out in the dark.
I will send fire
to warm and encourage you.
I will be with you in the fire
and I will be with you in the cloud.

You will learn to eat new food
and find refuge in new places.
I will give you dreams in the desert
to guide you safely home to that place
you have not yet seen.

The stories you tell
one another around your fires
in the dark will make you
strong and wise.

Outsiders will attack you,
and some who follow you,
and at times you will weary
and turn on each other

from fear and fatigue and
blind forgetfulness.

You have been preparing
for this for hundreds of years.
I am sending you into the wilderness
to make a way and to learn my ways
more deeply.

Those who fight you will teach you.
Those who fear you will strengthen you.
Those who follow you may forget you.
          Only be faithful.
          This alone matters.

Some of you will die in the desert,
for the way is longer than anyone
          imagined.
Some of you will give birth.

Some will join other tribes
along the way, and some
will simply stop and create
new families in a welcoming oasis.

Some of you will be so changed
by weathers and wanderings
that even your closest friends
will have to learn your features
as though for the first time.
Some of you will not change at all.

Some will be abandoned
by your dearest loves
and misunderstood by those
who have known you since birth
and feel abandoned by you.

Some will find new friendship
in unlikely faces, and old friends
as faithful and true
as the pillar of God's flame.

Wear protection.
Your flesh will be torn
as you make a path
with your bodies
through sharp tangles.
Wear protection.

Others who follow may deride
or forget the fools who first bled
where thorns once were, carrying them
away in their own flesh.

Such urgency as you now bear
may embarrass your children
who will know little of these times.

Sing songs as you go,
and hold close together.
You may at times grow
confused and lose your way.

Continue to call each other
by the names I've given you,
to help remember who you are.
You will get where you are going
by remembering who you are.

Touch each other
and keep telling the stories
of old bondage and of how
I delivered you.

Tell your children lest they forget
and fall into danger—remind them
even they were not born in freedom,
but under a bondage they no longer
remember, which is still with them,
if unseen.

Or they were born
in the open desert
where no signposts are.

Make maps as you go,
remembering the way back
from before you were born.

So long ago you fell
into slavery, slipped
into it unawares,
out of hunger and need.

You left your famished country
for freedom and food in a new land,
but you fell unconscious and passive,
and slavery overtook you as you fell
asleep in the ease of your life.

You no longer told stories
of home to remember
who you were.

Do not let your children sleep
through the journey's hardship.
Keep them awake and walking
on their own feet so that you both
remain strong and on course.

So you will be only
the first of many waves
of deliverance on these
desert seas.

It is the first of many
beginnings—your Paschaltide.
Remain true to this mystery.

Pass on the whole story.
I spared you all
by calling you forth
from your chains.

Do not go back.

I am with you now
and I am waiting for you.

Reclaiming the Feminine within Our Religious Traditions

Many women, perhaps most of us, begin our spiritual journey by trying to reclaim women's visibility, voice, role, and stories within our own tradition. This is an important step in all liberation movements. Keeping people divided from their history is a way of keeping them enchained.

I have long been fascinated by the dichotomy between religious institutions where women's energies are used and valued within a community, and religious institutions where discrimination and cultural codes against women were taught and passed from generation to generation (most often by women). In 1879, when she was eighty years old, Elizabeth Cady Stanton began to write the Women's Bible because she believed that it was important to stop passing these codes and to reclaim our religious tradition. Today we continue that work.

As women began to study biblical and other religious texts, it became very clear that theology had developed from a male perspective. Women were excluded by male language and often made invisible. Women's subordination to male dominance is often taught explicitly in biblical texts. The problem was that, as Jewish and Christian women, we knew we were there! The men couldn't have been there without us. We looked for the fragments of women's stories. We searched midrash and folklore and oral traditions. We read alternative commentaries on scripture, and old documents for the stories that had been deleted. We broadened our fields to include archeology, anthropology and art history. And we began to employ our imagination and collective memories, to use group discussions, exercises, meditations and rituals to "re-member" our heritage. We told the story of Lot's Wife and gave her a name, Dolores, woman of sorrow. We told the story of Isaac from Sarah's perspective, and sang Sarah's Circle and danced the Dance of Miriam. We remembered Hulda and her teaching and prophesying within the temple walls and the Gate of Hulda that stands today in Jerusalem.

Today we are aware that as global women we share many different heritages. We remember our sisters in the United States who are re-claiming their roots within Native American, Afro-American, Spanish American and Eastern traditions, and women throughout the world who are insisting on full membership in their religious institutions.

Brother Jesus, Mother Christ, Sister Spirit to these wakening women, these human stars. (60″ × 70″) Oil on canvas. 1976.

I have portrayed the Mother Christ as a gigantic star full of light and energy. Within the folds of her cape and in her outstretched arms are her spirits, wakening women, human stars, small reflections of the primary light. Genesis tells us we are both male and female, created in the image of God; so both male and female are contained within the Godhead—God the Mother and God the Father. The heritage given women that God is only male (and, therefore, the male is God) is damaging to the female self-image. The equality of women needs the visual symbol of a particular, personal, divine woman in order that her thinking can then move out and beyond gender to the concept that the energy which created the universe is, indeed, beyond sexual labels.

Mother Christ, Sister Spirit

Christ! Thank God you
are no longer the husband/lover
icon of my inner eye
(any more than you should be
for the soul's good eros),
nor the towering Master, lowering Lord
of my early childhood sleep,
but have at last risen
within my self's reality,
One-Who-Simply-Is.

Brother Jesus, Mother Christ,
creation's climax loving me through incarnation:
you stand by without/within,
heal, nurture, strengthen,
making me possible as you are possible.

Creator, Savior, Spirit,
beyond gender yet encompassing all:
Mother Bear to this wild cub,
Brother Lion to this lamb
(or Brother Lamb to this lion);
most wonderful of all, Sister Spirit
to these wakening women, these human stars.

The Annunciation (108″ × 68″) Oil on canvas. 1976.

Song of Mary

In the Age of the Molten Moon, Mary the Beloved gives birth.

My body chosen for Mystery, born to encompass the Holy One. How can this be? I, mere woman, made to form the Very One from the clay of my flesh, bone of my bone, nerve of my marrow, the heartbeat of God in my belly.

O Smallest One, egg of my being, my own bold Maker! Who knows you or who can name you?

When I lived a fish in my mother's womb, I was joy to my parents, the pride of their years, faith in a dying age. Early, perhaps too early, they returned me to you: back to the Temple. How could I know you? Yet I was yours, yours only.

A growing girl, a healthy child, I joyed in the sun with the muscle of work and the pride of my limbs. I ran with the wind, walked naked in rain, exulting with wings in my skin. When others laughed I laughed right back, yours only. *I was thine, I was born for thee; what was thy will with me?*

A young woman's voice came out of my body, quick in my days. My hair was black, silvered young by the sun, it streaked round my face, a gathering of lights. I am Virgin: woman-whole-unto-myself, no one's possession. The spirit in me, in my arms and hands, in the feet of my going, will praise thee.

O Hokmah! O Shekinah! I am the Temple of God, the Seat of the Covenant, the Ark of the Promise, the Lap of Creation. I am the Throne of the Universe, mother of millions. God's covenant with me in all creatures is honored. The Uncreated One has shown in my bones. Hear them crack in this birthing! This human form of dust and sun: we make God out of me. Like roots out of trees above ground I myself grow out of me: the honey flows out of me, a festival of bees. O Ruach! O Hokmah!

Wisdom be attentive: I claim thee.

My grandmothers feared to stray from their homes when young girls, lest a spirit creep from the cracks of the earth, under rocks, around weeds, to nest in their wombs. Was it when I bathed in the running river or lay honey-eyed in moonlight on hot summer nights? Did you come down some silver beam or out of the tree trunk beneath me in a flurry of bees? In a shower of gold or when I made love with words in my heart's poem? That time in prayer I saw the angel made of light in a fiery bower? O Being-made-of-motion faster than the earth, a streak, a lightning bolt, pure power in a moving shell: your gaze is laser, your color beyond the spectrum of our sight.

> Behold! I bear Power,
> All Power in my rounded shell,
> breath of my breath,
> being of my bones.
> Make room!
> Make fire! Strike flame!
> Light the earth.
> I bear Power.

What made you think me safe-and-humble when I am humble-full-of-Grace-and-Power. Do you not know that my body could go up in smoke and take you, this planet, take all heaven in its thunder? Call me Mother Thunder.

I carry lightning in my tender boom.

In this painting I portray the energy of conception as a new life placed within the womb of Mary. This reflects my personal feelings that the beginning of all new life is miraculous and charged with tremendous energy.

Nativity: Birth of the Sacrificial Lamb (84″ × 72″) Oil on canvas. 1976.

The Christ Child is portrayed as pure light and energy. The light and energy radiating from Mary are symbolic of her joy in the infant—not unlike the personal joy I felt at the birth of each of my own children and, indeed, the universal love and delight common to all mothers contemplating their new-born.

The cave of his birthplace is representative of the great feminine womb of the Earth from which all life comes and to which it eventually returns. The manger shape is remindful of an altar with the sacrificial victim already placed upon it. There is a cross-shaped supporting beam, another foreshadowing of Good Friday. It is, however, a living cross covered with roses (legend says roses bloomed wherever the Holy Family stopped during the flight into Egypt). They are said to have blossomed at the Nativity, closed at the Crucifixion, and reopened at Easter.

My body
is a land
of fruitful
vines and branches,
flowing
with milk and honey,
fertile with wine
that pours forth
with the turn
of the moon. . . .

from "Welcome Song"

Gloria

Light wisps low over Earth
at the crying of your birth,
a world cast on the face of night
become bright, bent childlike
beneath winter's feather of a moon.

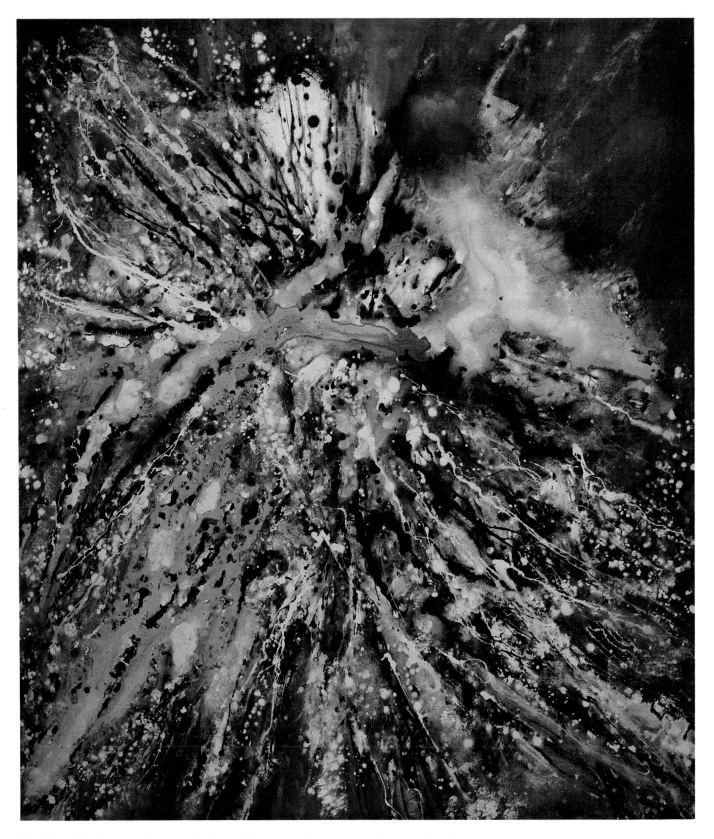

"Spirit of God, moved upon the face of the water." Genesis 1:2 (63″ × 67″) Oil on canvas. 1976.

This is my own personal iconograph of the Godhead—composed of light and energy and abstract in shape.

God Is a Verb

God
is
a
verb

God is one
mighty
roaring
verb

God is
One

God is
Mighty

God is
Roaring

God is
a Verb
roaring

God Is.

This verb named God
we now name New Being
solar lunar sidereal
motion soaring
breathing   burning   lightning
ultrasonic
SOUND

God is in us
we know,
being new,
stretch, strike, light-
ning soar-sound.

Godlike, sometimes we
just have to
rise up and
ROAR.

Mary, Hokmah: Goddess of Wisdom. (108″ × 66″) Oil on canvas. 1976.

Shekinah

Morning. An empty upper room.
In the golden mosque
over King David's Tomb,
the singing in tongues
of all the birds of the world,
lifting up languages in varied tones:
eagle, seagull, osprey, owl,
and under, the pure drone of honey-
bees, but all, voices with wing,
with quick, fluttering hearts,
fast and fastening eyes,
praying birds and birds of prey,
worshippers overcome in a holy place.

Now barefooted and veiled
on ancient stone, I join
the song, my bones hum happily
with the free singing of Israeli birds
here where Jews broke bread
for Pesach and Chaburah,
where the body of Earth
in bread showed itself
as the body of God,
and Her red blood poured
out among friends in the wine
and the dance and the dark-
deep silence.

So I remove the lavender blue
and silver-streaked veil,
hang its fringe from my hips, let light
encircle my waist and take me, take me,
dark hair falling gold on the lap of stone
on which my body breaks open, the bread
of the world.   I dance
in flowing time, dark of the moon
still coming, let blood fall easily
where they feasted, and Allah's children
prayed, and now I bring back Thanks
and dance for You, body of light
in sun's outpouring, I let my arms
become wings, my legs Your loving
limbs, dear mother, Jerusalem of Earth—
I am the goddess again, brightly dark
Queen of Judah praised by God,
I am Shekinah, and I dance for You!

The Cross of Joan of Arc (72″ × 72″) Oil and acrylic enamel
on canvas. 1978.

*This canvas is split into quadrants, each representing the living spirit
in four contemporary female theologians whose lives have been touched
by the sacrifice of St. Joan: Sister Judith Stoughton, C.S.J.; the Reverend Jeannette Piccard; the Reverend Alla Bozarth; and the Reverend
Mary Belfry.*

Godmothers of a New Creation

marking the twelfth anniversary of the Philadelphia
ordinations: to a new generation

We now proclaim the Story
valid and worthwhile.
A dozen years ago
we twelve-less-one,
unbetrayed by taking
history in our hands,
made and shaped a future
in faith and fear
for unknown others.
Now see, our blood
glistens in Easter light.

Now you are coming,
our daughters, descendants,
and you are worthy
of the price.

No longer the female patriarchs
of our fears or past years
(or now in the furnace
of our institutions),
you are women come of age,
seekers of life at the edge,
explorers of inner galaxies,
giving holiness again
to all that lives with
recognition in your eyes
and hands, true channels
of the healing power
of Mother/Father God.

And you are Wisdom Women,
daughters of Hokmah,
Ruach in your veins, Spirit
flowing like rivers through
your bodies' words,
prophetic fire still
shining in your faces.

You are old, young,
mothers, daughters,
sisters, lovers.
Not one unwounded
among you.

You bear the mark of the One
Who-gives-birth-with-blood,
Who-rises-wounded-and-gives-life
gently, intently, and truly
unrelenting of the gift
of Cosmos.

Now, our priesthood
having borne us by Grace
again and again through
harrows into heavens,
we stand large in
the Gate of Mystery,
with outstretched arms,
the Christic chalice
overflowing for all
that is new on the Earth.

Moment by moment we accept
our calling as midwife and mother,
healer and lover.
Together.

And so we who came before
now bless you who have come
and are coming, radiant
with God-pregnancy—
we bow before you,
ready and full,
Godmothers of a New Creation:

> May you bear well and rise,
> growing ever more
> loving and wise,
> strong from your life-giving
> wounds.

Red Dragon in Heaven (72″ × 72″) Oil on canvas. 1977.

This painting and the following one are part of a triptych entitled "The Bearers of the Sacred Bundles," which also includes the painting, "The White Buffalo Woman" (not shown). They all portray the essence of the Divine Feminine as She appeared to three different cultures bearing her gifts.

"God's temple in heaven was opened and the ark of his covenant was seen within his temple . . . and a great portent appeared in heaven, a woman clothed with the sun, with the moon under her feet, and on her head a crown of 12 stars. She was with child." Apocalypse of the New Testament 11:19, 12, 2. In the Old Testament, the ark of the covenant, the seat of the divine presence, the wisdom of God is Hokmah, which is a Hebrew word, feminine in gender. Hokmah, divine wisdom, is Mary of the New Testament. Great Mother, Lady of Life, Queen of Heaven, about to bring forth from her body the forces of good.

Dark Mother
Holy Protector
Snow Mountain Mother
Glorious Guide
Strong Succour
Eternal Friend
Woman Lover

Queen of Heaven
reigning in sun splendor,
Goddess of radiant power
armed with right passion,
the rage for justice
your shining shield,
saffron and gold
in red robes of fire
and pure light—
so reigns the Divine Mother. . . .

from "Liberation Song"

Guadalupe (48″ × 72″) Oil on canvas. 1989.

Guadalupe

"Juan Diego, what happened to you
that winter day running up the mountainside
to visit the sick old man?
What caught you, took you, changed you
through your eyes?
How could it be She, the One
I've waited decades to see
with faithfully downcast gaze?

"I was Her priest, Juan Diego,
Her son, Her servant,
I served Her from kings' palaces
and earthen shrines, fasted,
prayed, deprived my Spaniard's soul
of the body's light, to be worthy
of Her, Divine Mother, my spirit's
lover—Why, then, did She pass me by,
stop you there, Indian boy, bare feet
on dirty snow, when I would have kissed
Her feet with my tears and bathed
Her hands in my blood?

"If She comes to you again, Juan,
tell Her for me She is mistaken,
the gold shrine I've kept empty
for Her is here in the church, not
out there in the cold poor earth
of your unbooked people—
tell Her for me She is wrong!"

"Good Father, I told Her, I gave Her
your message. She said to tell you
it is for double healing that She comes
to the poor on this Mountain, the Ancient
Madre whose people prayed here thousands
of years before you. Her shrine is this
Mountain, image of Her womb, the breast
which gives life to the Saviour, and we,
the poor Indians, are Her own holy child,
the saviours of many.

"She comes for the mothers and
grandmothers who will bring sick
children here in their arms with
blood-stained knees, to climb
in Her lap for healing—and here
She told me to give you, dear Father,
Her sacred bundle, a sign of re-membering,
for you and all men of power to come home
again to your Mother and learn Her ways
of harmony with Earth and make peace."

"O God! I know now Who You Are!
The boy brought me Your sacred Gift,
the roses, roses everywhere, heavy
on me with heavenly beauty, this burden
I bear forever now, knowing all that
I've cherished is dross: personal pride
in my self-chosen suffering, hatred
of Your Body the Earth, hatred of Life!
Forgive me, Mother!

"I give You my life, I take Your holy
people in my arms, I abandon my safe
sanctuary and with these hands
from now on I will serve, I will
feed Your poor and kiss Your feet
in this unkempt boy's, and
rebuild You a home on Your Earth!"

The apparition of Guadalupe appeared on the Mexican site of an ancient Aztec temple dedicated to the goddess Tonantsi (our lady mother). The apparition told the Indian boy, Juan Diego, that her name was "Coattolopeuh." The Mexicans translated this to "Guadalupe," the dark virgin of Spain. Her sacred bundle of roses blooming in the snow and the magical imprint on her robe were symbols of divinity to the bishop who ordered a cathedral built on the site to honor Guadalupe's appearance.

Vision of St. Margaret Mary of Alocoque (83″ × 61″) Oil
on canvas. 1976.

"Jesus appeared to me. He was a blaze of glory—his five wounds shining like five suns, flames issuing from all parts of his human form, especially from his divine breast, which was like a furnace." Vision of St. Margaret Mary of Alocoque.

I have shown the energy and light of the five wounds of Christ as equal to the energy of five suns. It is my hope that the positive energy released into the world by his sacrifice will outweigh the energies of evil. It is my personal icon for the ultimate salvation of planet Earth as the home for humanity and the ceasing of nuclear madness.

Crosses

intersecting
upon Fire.

There are many dyings
but one Death

and many births
but one Resurrection.

Pearls

To women aware in male institutions.

You are pearls:
you began
as irritants.

The ocean pushed
your small, nearly
invisible
rough body
through an undetected
crack in the shell.
You got inside.

Happy to have a home
at last
you grew close
to the host,
nuzzling up
to the larger body.

You became
a subject
for diagnosis:
invader, tumor.

Perhaps your parents
were the true invaders
and you were born
in the shell—
no difference—
called an outsider
still.

You were a representative
of the whole
outside world,
a grain of sand,
particle of the Universe,
part of Earth.
You were a *growth*.

And you did not go away.

In time
you grew
so large,
an internal
luminescence,

that the shell
could contain
neither you nor itself,
and because of you
the shell Opened itself
to the world.

Then your beauty
was seen
and prized,

your variety valued:
precious, precious,
a hard bubble of light:
silver, white, ivory,
or baroque.

If you are a specially
irregular and rough
pearl, named baroque
(for broke),
then you reveal
in your own
amazed/amazing
body of light
all the colors
of the universe.

Reclaiming the Goddess in History

From art images, the earliest records that humans have left us, we know that we first envisioned God/Goddess as female. For 25,000 years of art history, the Creatress of All was seen and imaged as woman. Only in Western culture in the last 1,500 years has God been only male—and even there the images of Mary as a central figure appear repeatedly. In Jewish tradition the images of the Shekinah, God's presence, and the Queen of the Sabbath, represent the female principle. This information can have profound impact on women and men today. The Goddess appears all over the known world. In some places she is the central figure; in others she shares her powers, sometimes with her daughter, other women, or her brother, spouse, or son. She has many faces, shapes and stories. The Great Mother is seen as Creatress of All Life and Civilization. She—the Chaos, the Salt Waters, the Sea—divides herself into the Mother Earth and all of its creatures. She is the Giver of food, water, and the air that nurture all human, animal and plant life. She brings all the Gifts of Civilization—Fire, Language, Grain, Art, Dance, Music, Writing. She is the symbol of Life Force itself, not only a biological mother. She is part of and one with all Living Things.

The information about the Goddess and her images is filled with paradox and limitations. She seldom represents power over or perfection. She usually represents life forces or the celebration of life and fertility. In a paradox two opposites can both be true. This reframes the dualistic, either/or thinking. The Goddess is the Giver of Life and Death; she is Maiden/Mother/Crone—all part of the same continuum.

Knowing about the Goddess and her history tells us that patriarchy has only been in existence a short time—that as individuals and as a culture we have choices in how we decide to image God. This can have enormous political and psychological implications. Contemporary women are finding great potential for healing in Goddess images. And contemporary artists are creating new images. Perhaps one of the most important reasons for women to research Goddess history (and the history of spirituality and religion) is that here is one of the clearest paths to track the development of patriarchy and war-culture values.

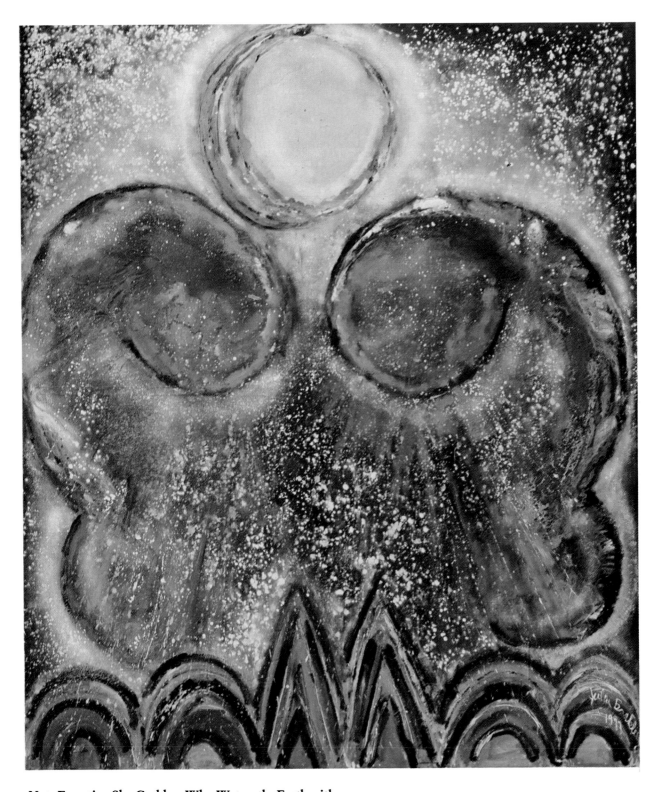

**Nut: Egyptian Sky Goddess Who Waters the Earth with
Her Rain-Milk** (60″ × 70″) Oil on canvas. 1976.

Mother with the Moon in Your Mouth

Sitting by the Maiden Well
with your host of pigs
suckling and grunting,
goddess of spring-to-life,
White Sow Goddess
rolling with desire
in the hay mounds
in the Age of the Molten Moon,
Ishtar, goddess of underdeath,
the moon rising in the east
over places of burial and birth

omphalos flowers resting
in their hollowed nest,
a bee making honey
from earth's bellyhole

your life shines
and even the Laughless Rock
rocks with laughter,
cracks and rocks,
unable to attend
your magic.

You, Woman Impervious,
Moon Stuck in Her Throat,
teach me the old ways,
put me to sleep
with the old magic.
Make stars rise
on my breasts
like silver women
dancing naked
encircled by night
by a legion of wings.

From ages of Ages
arise from the dark,
the flash of your buckle,
the beat of your braceleted
arms on our breasts,
Moon Mother and Maiden, Awake!

Bakerwoman God

Bakerwoman God,
I am your living bread.
Strong, brown Bakerwoman God,
I am your low, soft, and being-
shaped loaf.
I am your rising
bread, well-kneaded
by some divine and knotty
pair of knuckles,
by your warm earth hands.
I am bread well-kneaded.

Put me in fire, Bakerwoman God,
put me in your own bright fire.

I am warm, warm as you from fire.
I am white and gold, soft and hard,
brown and round.
I am so warm from fire.

Break me, Bakerwoman God.
I am broken under your caring Word.
Drop me in your special juice in pieces.
Drop me in your blood.
Drunken me in the great red flood.
Self-giving chalice swallow me.
My skin shines in the divine wine.
My face is cup-covered and I drown.

I fall up
in a red pool
in a gold world
where your warm
sunskin hand
in there to catch
and hold me.
Bakerwoman God,
remake me.

"The Sea Leapt from the Abyss Where It Was Formed as a Child in Its Mother's Womb." (60" × 70") Oil on canvas. 1975.

"The Mother of our world seed bore us in the beginning. She is the Mother of all races . . . and the Mother of all tribes. She is the Mother of thunder, the Mother of the rivers, the Mother of the trees and of all kinds of things. She is the Mother of the Milky Way. She is the Mother of the rain. She alone is the Mother of things, she alone."
                              from "Song of the Kagoba Indians"

These works ("The Sea Leapt . . ."; "Nut, the Egyptian Sky Goddess . . ."; "River Goddess . . ."; and "Astarte . . .") portray the nurturing, life-giving forces of nature as female. They are an exploration of the archetype of the Great Mother, the inward Feminine image found in the collective mytholgies of all people and in the human psyche. These historical female deities reflect my conviction that the ultimate is feminine as well as masculine.

Mama Sea and Mama Rock

A haystack in the ocean?
A granite mound of seaweed straw?
No—a sea goddess,
Mother of the Sea Beasts, rising
for earth and sea children's play.
Oh, the sea frolic of it!
The cavorting on her toes!
Bicycles in ten speeds and sizes
awobble in sand, the wiggles
of Piscean feet let free in the seaground,
erotic dreams of stallions agallop
in spindrift, the leaping legs
of young dogs giddily dancing
after kites, whose foil rainbow tails
twirl through clouds, bright shadows
left on the sky for shooting stars to follow.
The goddess rises, and plays, healed
from old memories of burial at sea,
old losses forgotten in the furrows of her wings.
We climb them and suckle.
She is a breast, a bird, a great mother whale,
old wise woman with mossy kelp hair,
ornamental seagulls are moving white flowers
that sing in her hair—

And the great sea tickle
at her knees, the cosmic applause
of surf for her victories and ours,
the wailing of whales turning
from belly to back to sing
and laugh at this: all mutability,
changeless change.

A woman of twenty dreamily moves through foam,
not lifting her feet, the soft disturbance
of lilac pleats in her skirt, the flowing
blonde down her back in the wind,
the guitar that is silent to wait for a song;
the woman of sixty arm in arm with her friend;
at sunset an old painter makes tracks with her cane;
and eighty year old lovers, their arms around each other,
aim straight for the depths, her bright red pantsuit
mocking the red flag on the beach for Danger Today.

I come here to the nest of my origins
on a summer morning,
seabound with a hot sea-hunger,
desperate with thirst for a mountain.
My life thrown open around all life,
full of mountain milk, at last I come
to this water, to drink and to die and give birth.
My eye is fed, and ocean soup, it is good.
Aphrodisiac of Earth!
I am free and fertile,
woman-with-poem again.

Oh, Mamas, I am here, and I see.
Stilled, I rock and rejoice
in the cradle of life you are.
Leaving the goddess rock to transform
herself into another planet or birth
a star, I move out.
Bowing into the surf
my body that is one
lifts into wave upon wave.
My blood is at home.
I hold the ocean in my arms.

River Goddess: Dispenser of Life (48″ × 48″) Oil on canvas. 1973.

From before history through the present, there are images of the Living Water, the sacredness of water that gives life. Honoring wells, springs, then larger streams and rivers is all part of honoring the River Goddess. Many rivers have been named for goddesses. The Boyne and Shannon Rivers of Ireland, for example, are said to have been named for the goddesses Boarn and Sinann. The Gaul goddess Sequanna was a deity of healing; the Seine River was named for her, and she was worshiped at this river's source.

From Here

From here
the river
is a ribbon
of light—

One rose,
the color
of bright
coral seashell,
blooms
in the autumn
yard

and the pasture
grass dazzles green
with new rain
and low sun

and October trees
find their true
color again
before death—

From here
the waterfall
roars
below me

and the brave sun
smells cool.

From here the river
is a ribbon of light
and the full moon
rests a moment
abreast the red summit
of White Mountain.

From here I almost know
the secret of the stars,
how small the Earth is,
my own way home.

Astarte: Lady of All Liberation (48″ × 60″) Oil on canvas.
1973.

Here she is depicted riding a lion, brandishing weapons with three of her arms.

. . .
Your heart beats
a song, a battle song,
a love song,
burning in your fiery
dark woman body,
in your full
woman beauty
chanting your
woman truth.

Mother of Life

Lion-rider
Sea-tamer
Skull-bearer
Fire-dancer
Holy Destroyer

Lady of All Liberation

purge our souls
of the world's woe,
prepare us for victory!

from "Liberation Song"

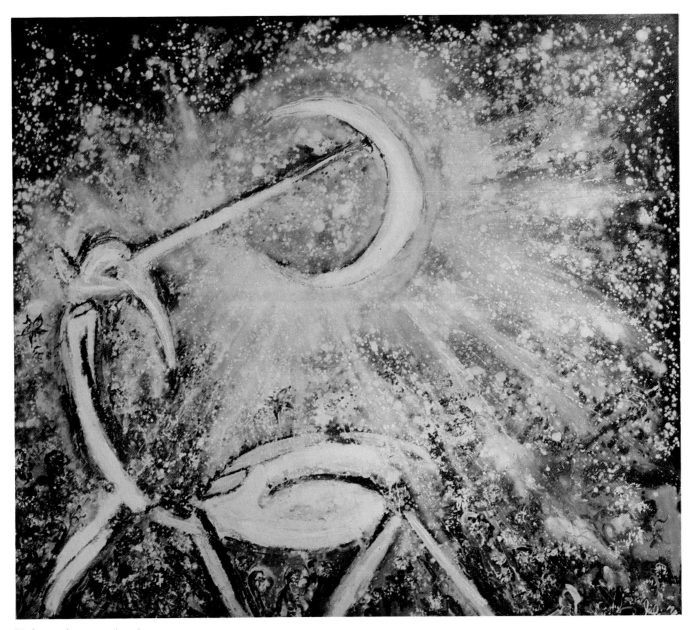

Unicorn (68″ × 60″) Oil on canvas. 1975.

For Julia

A Christmas gift of free
flying lessons your children
thought you'd like—

Grandmother Magic upon them!
You're way past planes—

Don't they know you ride
on golden unicorns and fly
with bright green dream dragons?

Moon Priest

I am wicca, wise woman,
welcomed sister
to water and wood;
night's child,
I fear no flight
down village streets;
on Full Moon Night
I climb a star ladder
to see over the edge
of other galaxies.

By Dark of the Moon
I crawl into chimneys
and go straight up
in smoke,
disembodied
by Utter Dark,
and on the morning
of the New Moon
my neighbors complain
of a wind
that kept them
awake.

When thunder comes
I am lightning
in my silver
gown.
I run barefoot in rain,
crying, madly in love,
until my lover

the white unicorn
catches me
on his golden horn
and takes off

on the power
of our loving
union.

Violet and red
with our speed,
we ride skyclad
in fire, eagle and bear,
comet and star.

Then I am
Winged Woman.

Five Fertility Figures (60″ × 108″) Oil on canvas. 1987.

Drawing on aboriginal African art forms, Picasso savagely gave the world an expression of his contempt for the female and his own raw sexuality in his painting "Les Demoiselles d'Avignon" ("five horrifying women, prostitutes who repel rather than attract and whose faces are primitive masks.") In this painting, I am drawing on aboriginal Native American art forms and celebrating the life-giving fertility of the female as an expression of my own sexuality (mother of five, grandmother of fourteen).

You Need to Know

A Nuclear Age love poem based on the idea that war
is the outcome of pregnancy envy.

If birth is the realm of the mothers,
then death is the domain of the fathers.
The Patriarchal Phallicy

You need to know that we are
life-bearers but your role,
though subtle, is also essential:
with us you are love-makers
and life-givers.

So lay aside your self-defense
construct, death-bearer projectiles
erected everywhere on Earth's round
belly, inside her waters, and your
intellectual machismo lording it
over and over each other and us
in language, in image, in church
and state and school and work and play,
and lay down your weapon of flesh
and lie beside the woman, your partner,

beloved other, each other's teacher,
and remember your work and play—
your true religion—is to love together
and to love life into new being knowing
your role in this is not inferior and needs
no lead or steel cover-up with words
or will or weapons.

And then rise up with the one
you learn to love
to nurture true independence
in yourself and each other,
and draw out the gifted
more than the giver,
and worship what lives
by loving on and on and on . . .

Three Goddess Chromatics

White for the Virgin
Red for the Mother
Black for the Crone

(We speak the language of our conquerors)

white for the morning
the color of open
the color of waiting
the color of expectation
the Ready color:
I am Unpossessed Young Woman

red the color of gift
of outpouring of life
the bloodflower of being woman
the mother-flow mandala
painted by the paint of our bodies
the lifeflower the mystical rose:
I am Mother Many-color

black the color of All-colors
black the wise-Old
black the gift of time
black the blending
of gold with sun, earth,
night, black-the-beautiful-
and-whole:
I am Crone

We Three Full
in our own time,
fine together

No Longer
do we speak the speech of Usurpation

We claim All
the old tongues of colors, colors
of night, light, fire, flowers
the chromatic music
rose plum purple mauve
red ruby crimson carmine
our Own good colors

We speak our language old
and new and it is Colorful
(it is subtle) (it is pro-gressive)
        (it is Good)
              and
              it is

OURS

The Goddess Within: Celebrating Women's Lives

While women have been very excited about finding ancient archeological and historical goddess images, most women do not want to return to centuries- or millennia-old religions. Instead they are exploring the Goddess Within and the possibilities that open in seeing God in a female form. The goddess images revalidate women's bodies, life experiences, stories, history and the right to power.

Women have been damaged in many ways by living in a patriarchal system. We lost our identity, and many of us learned to hate being women. We have learned to trivialize ourselves and other women, to deny our bodies and to be unsatisfied with them, to accept institutionalized violence in silence—including economic and physical battering, rape and incest within the nuclear family. We have been taught to blame ourselves and each other.

In Women's Spirituality, we celebrate the sacredness of women's bodies and their body processes. We reclaim our own sexuality. We tell each other the secrets of pain and violence in our lives. We re-value women's friendships. We reclaim our powers of creativity in art, writing, storytelling, music, song and dance. We create rituals of celebration, healing and joy and reclaim our spiritual powers.

Virginal (68″ × 71″) Oil on canvas. 1973.

"Virginal" and "Female Synergy" (following) were both painted as part of a manifold series celebrating the female body. They are worked in assigned, intensified colors and expressionist brush strokes to reflect my joy in my femaleness.

Virginal

virgin: a woman in her own possession

Beloved,
I do not need you
for my wholeness;
I want you
for my joy.

Loving the Body

I have lost my place.
My body has become
a foreign country.
I no longer know
its maps or rules.

What languages it speaks
are silent to me or
frighten me to silence
by their strangeness.

They seem harsh.
They come from nerve,
and grate.

Even muscle groans
under their sounds.
Skin erupts in the effort
of trying to understand.

I am dried out
from loss of tears.
And sometimes
there are screams.

I grow suddenly dizzy,
caught in the white-out
of an inner tundra storm.
Without focus I cannot tell
if I am going somewhere
or holding still.

I want to move freely
in this country and
live here again.
I want to respond well
to its voices and weathers,
learn its new laws.
I want to feel its welcome again.
I want to be unafraid and peaceful
and know that, after all,
I was born here.

I need an interpreter in my own skin.
Friend, help me to find and keep place here.
Be doctor or lover.
Hold me, and remind me how.

Female Synergy (48″ × 48″) Oil on canvas. 1973.

Gynergy

for Antonia Brico on my thirtieth birthday

I have been asleep for ten years of my life
but today am waking, waking

aware of the seahorse
alone in his quiet lair
the male-mother who gives birth
laboriously in salt water

and aware of the male nanny grebe
who cares for the kids
while mother bird tests
her wings against the sun
for food to feed their young

aware also of the countless gifts
of female energy that would
surely explode the world
if they were known,
and go wasted as if to spare
the planet, but instead
the planet dies with them

aware of the beauty of old
women's hands on young women's
shoulders who take to the fluid
process of science, paint, or poetry,
or pound out their magic music
on primitive drums, on strings,
through horns sending their lusty wail:
for life! for life!

Aware of these forces I wake
out of my middle years
to look into the infinite eyes
of my sisters, daughters,
mothers, grand and godmothers,
caught in their endless
circle of energy, created anew
in their nurture, begin to see
the vast deep roots of my woman nature
reaching around the earth and held
in their circular fire
with great white waters
running under,

and wonder for wonder,
how I shall ever sleep again.

[N.B. Synergy: a physical law describing a composite energy which says that the whole is greater than the sum of its parts. Gynergy is female synergy.]

Sisterhood Is Synergy

Sisterhood is the affirmation
of being against nonbeing.
It is a corporate No
to the collective lie
of our unimportance.
Sisterhood is powerful
because we say No to the life-denying
structures of society
and Yes to the New Being we are becoming.
Sisterhood is powerful
because to live always on the edge
is dangerous, and to fully accept
the absolute ambiguity of our own reality
is hard.
To accept the reality of our being
over against the illusory nonbeing
of alien structures is not only
hardpain and crazypain,
but necessary and vitally creative.
Sisterhood is powerful
because to survive we have to
be constantly moving
in and out of our own minds
and this is fearsome.
Sisterhood is powerful
because the opposite of sorority is nonentity.
Sisterhood is synergy
because we together are richer
and greater and stronger and more power-full
than the sum of all other parts;
we are more powerful than ourselves
and we are ourselves.
Sisterhood is powerful
because we are broken parts in an invincible whole,
and each one of us *is* that whole.

Ninth Month (66″ × 67″) Oil on canvas. 1973.

Though I count the birthing and rearing of my five children as the most fulfilling part of my life, I never enjoyed the physical state of pregnancy, especially the ninth month.

Not at Home
for Julia

Sometimes love leads to birth.
Sometimes love leads to death.

She could barely remember
how she got into this.
It happened when she was
someone else—younger,
much younger, flat-bellied
and foreign, taken off-guard
between paintings of Genesis
and Armagedon, which were
one and the same in her dreams.

Now she sits here
in her ninth month,
a head on top of this mound
that used to be her body
but no more resembles her
than the Statue of Liberty—
big and stuck and unfree.

She's forgotten everything:
how to talk to friends,
how to read or walk or run,
how to drive,
how to play tennis,
how to play cards,
how to paint,
how to make love.

But oddly, though before
all this she couldn't swim,
she finds herself an expert
floater, a skill that does her
no good, for she's too bulky
for the tub and too tired
for big water—not getting in
but getting undressed for it.

So she sits here naked
in this red chair
trying to remember
how she got this way
and whether or not she knew
to avoid it.

Perhaps, after all,
something . . .
will come
of it.

Conjugal Capers (68″ × 67″) Oil on canvas. 1973.

"Marriage rage, martial art, mar us all."
from "Out of the Corner Not Fighting"

Out of the Corner Not Fighting

martial love
marital law
have us all up
against the wall
and cornered and
preserve the species
of the beast in all of us

marriage rage
martial art
mar us all

mythic misses
such as
poet/poetess
adult/adultress
have got to go
for us to come
of age

going going gone
well. Here we are,
two kinds of humankind
more one and more two
than we ever knew,
coming into our own
and off each other's backs at last.

Love Mantra for Letting Go

I bless you
I release you

I set you free
I set me free

I let you be
I let me be.

Heliotrope Bouquet Rag (72″ × 96″ and 60 pounds!) Oil on
canvas. 1975.

This painting depicts the energy of ragtime music. A dancer moves to
the ragtime beat of Heliotrope Bouquet. It is part of a twenty-three-
painting series.

Women at Play

Alice and Alla

Tuesday afternoons, a sunporch reveille
of women: sixty years between them,
elbow to elbow they sit at the piano,
playing together.

Their names mean Truth and Essence.
The ninety year old physician,
the thirty year old priest,
pioneers in their times,
healers in their ways,
take their own time
to rest under music's wings.

The singing Dove enfolds them,
and the keys their fingers touch
open to them such refreshment,
they feast themselves on light.
The younger one sits to the right in shadow,
the elder inclines left toward the window.
When no mistake is made
their hands overlap,
often little fingers are startled
to be on the same key,
releasing the sound doubly.

Vivace! O joy—
the power held in Adagio,
teased out in Allegro, set free
at the end when the brittle
arthritic bones leap over
wedding rings on smoother hands
to a Finale of pure praise.
The crossing of two lives.

And for both, honestly, relief
that for another week
they have survived and triumphed
through error all the way
to the end.

"You must live to be one hundred,"
says the child, "so we can be
good enough with practice to play
for our friends and family."
"Agreed. It will take that long!"

In summer, neighbors wonder
through the open windows how
they never tire of the same
First Symphony.

Adjourned to the kitchen for tea
the two conjecture and make kind
personal remarks about Herr Beethoven,
placating him in case from his place
in the communion of saints he has overheard
the preceding debacle.

Then the mutual exchange of stories:
work, travel, interesting friends, colorful authors.
And flowers out the window sparkle
in the golden afternoon's recessive beauty.
Within, amber butterflies on white wallpaper
dance about their heads as they laugh,
peel peaches together, sip tea, and admire
the good sense of a God who allowed
their times to overlap, their differences
to dissolve in the play that makes them
true contemporaries.

The hour passes and each has forgotten
which is the elder or younger,
whose memory embraces what wars or weddings.
Only the moment, clear and alive,
remains a constant fragile gift.

Each week's goodbye reveals
unspoken understanding and the abiding
gratitude of two hearts on loan to each other.

Some of Us Walk on Water (108″ × 68″) Oil on canvas.
1976.

"Some of Us Walk on Water" is my interpretation of the sea of change and the resulting tempest that women have experienced during the last three decades in the feminist desire for change and equality. I was born, raised and married in an era when women were "seen and not heard." I was middle aged before I first picked up a paint brush to chronicle all the incredible changes that were occuring in my life and the lives of women around me. To be able to say all of the things—with my brush—that were formerly forbidden for me to say, has been an experience of greatest joy. Women have truly walked on water to overcome.

Water Women

We do not want
to rock the boat,
you say, mistaking
our new poise
for something safe.

We smile secretly
at each other,
sharing the reality
that for some time
we have not been
in the boat.

We jumped
or were pushed
or fell
and some leaped
overboard.

Our bodies form
a freedom fleet,
our dolphin grace
is power.

We learn and teach
and as we go
each woman sings;
each woman's hands
are water wings.

Some of us have become
mermaids or Amazon whales
and are swimming for our lives.

Some of us do not know how to swim.
We walk on water.

Religious Manifesto of a Grown Woman:
A Personal Re-Membering

A Sunday afternoon twilight
raining outside doesn't know
if it's winter or spring,
thunderstorm springing
out of blizzard's belly.

Inside, I am reading about Goddesses:

Daughter Mother and Crone Goddesses
Isis Asherah and Demeter
Kali Persephone and Hecate
The usual, and not a few new.

Memories in the midst of their naming
float up in the dim din.
I see my mother in an old kitchen
turning and turning the cup
getting the first and last mouthful
of amber always from the saucer.
Then she reads the tea leaves.
She is always more accurate
than anyone dares to admit.

I see her reading the cards
decades before Tarot was popular,
throwing coins and marked sticks
when her civilized neighbors (and
this was in New York City) had never
heard of the I Ching.

I see her before I was born
divining my sex, summoning my gender.
Her name was the same as mine—*Alla*—
not the only gift I divine my mother
gave to me.

Old and prudish at fifteen
(taking after, then, my formerly
Methodist father), she told me
our Russian name meant goddess.
I blushed and never spoke of it
out loud, telling others the story
I'd contrived that it was short for *Alleluia,*
claiming always, then, only half my heritage.

At twenty-five she muttered
to me truths about my dead grandfather
I was still too young to hear
and called in delirium for her Gypsy
teacher from the old days of her
Black Sea girlhood, forest friend.
I pretended not to hear and turned,
waiting for her to return.
She never came back to me

until a few years ago in my
finally humbled own maturity
one night as I lay bellydown
on the floor drinking Caravan tea
propped on leaves of cards
at my elbows, humming and waking
the night into Pentacles,
Wands, Cups, and Swords,
seeing myself amazed in the Major Arcana,
healing with fingers like psychic lightning rods.
Now my students call my methods
magical and strange—friends say
my habits are increasingly outrageous
and name me with such epithets
as Witch, Elf, Daughter of Inanna, Sorcerer,
Magic Mother, Virgin Priestess, Shameless Hussy,
    Shaman.

O Mother, forgive me the stupidity
of my youth by which I betrayed us both.
I can say it now. I can say, proudly,
Mama, I'm as crazy as you,
and I have my own secrets
which I keep from the authorities.

I can name the truth in our name
that flows dangerously in our bones and veins:

I am Alla
I am Goddess
Alleluia

Facing Oppression

This is perhaps the hardest part of the journey, the crossroads where many turn back. This is the place where many people close their eyes and refuse to see, to know what they know, because it is too painful. In the Twelve Steps of Alcoholics Anonymous, Al-Anon, and in other recovery programs, people learn that we must first acknowledge the problem if we are to break through the denial systems we have set up and change the oppressive hold that addictions and destructive thinking patterns have in our lives.

We live in a world that holds and supports war-culture values that began developing 6,000 years ago in dominant, hierarchal warrior societies. Patriarchy is a system of power over, hierarchy and dominance, supported by intimidation, violence and fear. We can catch glimpses of other ways of organizing ourselves on this earth in paleolithic and neolithic and early historical art and from some contemporary indigenous peoples, who live in peaceful, egalitarian ways.

We must acknowledge our global systems of oppression—sexism, racism, heterosexism, classism, colonialism, imperialism, warfare, greed, our destruction of our earth, her creatures and her resources if we are to start our steps toward healing. We must see the connections between these oppressions if we are to create a world of equality, liberation and peace. For many women, the burning of some six to nine million women as witches between 1400 and 1700 C.E. (Common Era) symbolizes Western culture's hatred of women. The word witch is derived from wicca, meaning Wise Woman. These women were healers, herbalists, midwives and spiritual guides. Christian women are appalled that these atrocities—like many religious wars in our time—were committed in the name of organized religion.

Today, Roman Catholic women are still denied ordination and the right to perform sacraments. Women in other religious traditions are still meeting discrimination of many kinds. The statistics on wife battering and child abuse are staggering in our so-called civilization. Many women are still told by court systems and counselors in both church and community settings that they are at fault. And even when a woman is faced with an abusive marriage and manages to leave it, she is severely penalized economically. Poverty is a women's issue.

Nuclear warfare is a totally new concept that makes the old values of power over obsolete. No one can win in a nuclear war. It kills not only those present but the unborn children, other creatures and the food chain as well. Sister Miriam MacGillis from Global Perspectives says that Chernobyl teaches us that there are no boundaries or national lines.

We are the only humans to have seen our planet Earth from outer space. Sister Dorothy Olander with Global Education asks, "What do you see when you look at the posters of Earth from space?" Water, clouds, the earth. This image teaches us clearly that we all share the same planet Earth. What we do to our waters, our air and our land in one part of the Earth affects us all. State and national boundaries are human constructs. And we are a global people.

Travail

We women bear men
even though they cannot bear us.
We bear them over and over
as fathers, sons, and lovers.

May this ill-bearing end.
May they enter the Cosmic Womb
of the Great Mother and be
well born by Her once and for ever.

May they emerge as our brothers
and may we their mothers
become only their sisters and lovers.

This painting, from the "Circle of Fire" series, concerns the murder of an estimated nine million women for witchcraft during the Middle Ages. It was prompted by a performance piece of artist Mary Beth Edelson in which the names of burned women were chanted. One of those was Mary Barkley, burned at the stake by her father and four brothers for refusing to marry the man of their choice. Since I had a daughter with the same name, who also had four brothers, the chant and the horror of this killing stuck in my mind and started my research into this infamous murder of women as witches.

Contemporary scholars believe that in some villages nearly all the females were burned. They were executed on many pretexts, but the real reason was to destroy female power. One midwife, Agnes Simpson, was burned at the stake for relieving the pains of childbirth with laudanum. In Toulouse, France, four hundred women were burned to death in one day. Researching for this painting and others in the series was one of the most emotionally painful experiences of my life.

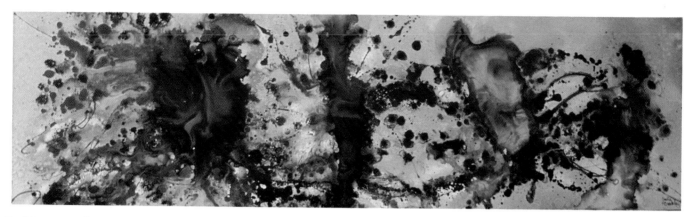

In Memory of Four Women of Perth, Burned at the Stake (36″ × 120″) Acrylic enamel on aluminum. 1976.

Wicca

"Have nothing
to do
with That Woman
for she is
A Witch"

the inquisitor writes
to the sacred teacher

"her body will
surely endanger
all men
and her mind
will undo
your mind."

The unholy seer
is blind.
He does not see
that womanly power
is power to heal,
that womanly magic
unbinds.
His chains are over his eyes.
He does not hear our cries.

He is weak now
and his word
no longer burns.

While we are women-in-travail
with God, yearning over creation,
grieving all desecrations
of our Earthmother's grand body,
bringing to birth her renewal
and ours.

And we are witches,
intending healing

for all the Living,
offering our being
that Life will survive—
Daughters of Eve
whose name means Alive!
We pour ourselves out
to form a connection
(that includes even him)
in harmonic passion
for the well-being
of All.

While the ancient Great Goddess
shines in our faces:
unpossessed,
life-giving
and wise,
Protector of birth,
life, death, and more
life—

You meant to call us wicked
but you only called us wise.

Circle of Fire

FOR THE NINE MILLION WOMEN KILLED

For having too-small feet, marks on their bodies, natural religion, desire toward their God, love of each other, ancient wisdom; for disobeying husbands, for thinking for themselves, for mystical flight; for not cooking/speaking/sewing pleasingly; for keeping silence; for not keeping silence; for refusing the use and abuse of their bodies and souls; for healing with herbs by natural laws; for ecstasy

AS WITCHES
for six hundred years in the Modern Era.

*   *   *

And the more they killed
US
the more
WE GREW

When the mother goes out
to her fields of wheat
to her fields of maze
to her fields of buckwheat
to her fields of rice
to her fields of flowers
when the mother goes out
will she return

And the more they killed
US
the more
WE GREW

When the daughter goes out
to her paths of honey
to her paths of brick
to her paths of labor
to her paths of play
to her wonderful paths of work
when the daughter goes out
will she return

And the more they killed
US
the more
WE GREW

When the grandmother goes out
to her colors of amber
to her colors of gold
to her colors of black
to her colors of crimson
to her beautiful rainbow colors
when the grandmother goes out
will she return

And the more they killed
US
the more
WE GREW

When the sister goes out
to her wide roads
to her yellow roads
to her roads of diamond
to her roads of coal
to her roads of cement
when the sister goes out
will she return

And the more they killed
US
the more
WE GREW

When the friend goes out
to her mines of emerald
to her mines of tin
to her mines of copper
to her mines of amethyst
to her mines of bodies
when the friend goes out
will she return

And the more they killed
       US
    the more
    WE GREW

The priests & prophets: We honor
The healers & heroes: We honor
The farmers & gardeners: We honor
The midwives & miners: We honor
The judges & geniuses: We honor
The astronomers & physicists: We honor
The teachers & poets: We honor
Their holy lives: We honor
Their courage to deviate
   from the subhuman norms
   expected of them:
     We honor
Their unjust deaths: We honor

The women accused: We Remember
The women burned: We Remember
The women shot: We Remember
The women torn: We Remember
The women pierced: We Remember
The women beaten: We Remember
The women flayed: We Remember
The women left unburied: We Remember
The women buried & forgotten: We
                 Remember

Until they live again NOTHING
    will grow

through every devastation
    we endure
through every desecration
    we endure
through every destruction
    we endure
through every desolation
    we endure

through every dishonor
    we endure
through every despicable
    MURDER
    we endure
through every horror
    we endure
through every harrowing
    we endure
through every blood-letting
    we endure
through every soul-spilling
    we endure

through every utter holocaust
    we endure
through every hidden history
    we endure
through every outrage of thunder
    we endure
through every circle of fire
    we endure

Unto Ages of Ages
    we endure

our blood endures
our body endures
our soul which is One endures
our spirit & will endure
our minds endure

WE ENDURE AND ENDURE AND ENDURE

When the living blood goes out
When the blood of holy women goes out
When the blood of happy women goes out
When the blood of nurturing women goes out
When the blood of NEEDED women goes out
When the blood of BELOVED women goes out
When the blood of BRAVE women goes out
When the blood of harried women goes out
When the blood of horrible women goes out
When the blood of wise old women goes out
When the blood of fierce young women goes out
When all the light in the world goes out
When the blood goes out
      of Us

WE ENDURE AND

WE SHALL RETURN!

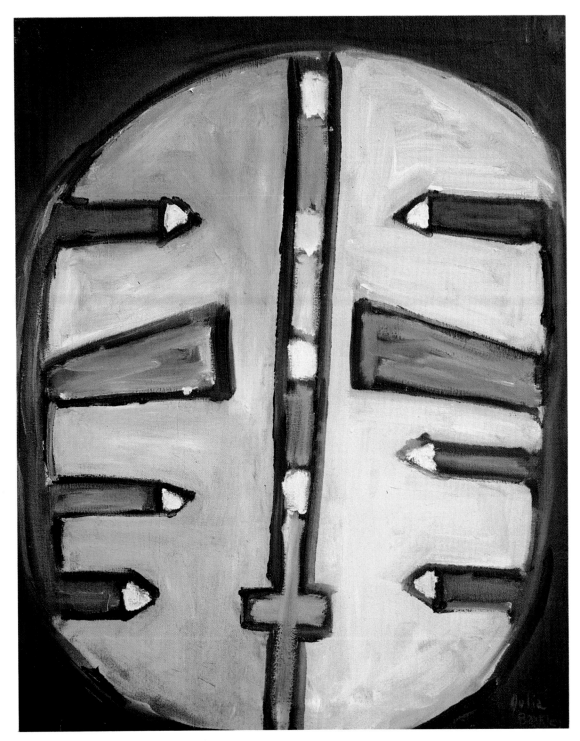

Phallic War Shield (24″ × 30″) Oil on canvas. 1989.

This war shield, carried by an ancient warrior, abounds in phallic symbolism used in this manner as a male talisman of strength-over, domination, vanquishing.

War Over Women

A genetic flaw
peculiar to gender—
initiation of the male
human into manhood
by aggression

forest or fortress
city or citadel
the skin peels back
blood surges, hair
rises, eyes bulge
then death—
hero and martyr are one.

Coming of age means
going to war.
Valour means victory
not honor, and glory
is gore. War games
at home or on foreign soil.
The undead are praised
the dead are buried.
Then celebration.

Peacemakers are first
target. War at all costs!
Viva! Viva! La muerte!
So from the beginning
men have loved war
more than women.

The thrill of pure hate
exceeds the joy of pure lust.
They need love and hate
their need and themselves
in their need,

compete for blood, bizarre
in the winning.

When will they love life
more than death, learn to live
lustily with grateful hearts?
When will men become peaceable
beings, come to love women
more than war?

War Shields (70″ × 50″) Oil on canvas. 1988.

I painted this canvas as a commentary on "an eye for an eye and a tooth for a tooth." It does not matter whether we make reference to aborigines with shields and spears or tanks in Flanders Fields or atom bombs on Hiroshima. Evil does not change all that much, just the means of its expression.

From Flanders Fields to Nevada

Evil exists,
fear-cum-hate,
militant ignorance
made arrogant—
original sin
the inclination
toward self-hate
projected outward
and then destroyed—

fear of not being
biggest, best,
meaning less than
nothing, bad
and weak and wrong.

Evil was clearer then,
when blood and mud
drowned daffodil bulbs
in Flanders Fields—
grey tanks spouted
the ultimate
male orgasm,
the colossal
erection towered
over other men,
then shuddered
backward and exploded
its seed of death
in a visible arc
over history—

Evil was clearer then.
Now in shame, more subtle,
underground, hidden,
it takes another form—
it goes inside
the body of Mother Earth,
the souls of men,
it kills from within.

Rape Poem
Death Koan: The Sound of One Hand

Clapping.
What is the sound of a woman's head bleeding
What is the sound of muscle tearing
What is the sound of semen greening
What is the sound of the trickle of blood across a thigh
        of semen on blood trickling
What is the sound of hate in the form of flesh
What is the sound of half a clap or half a scream
What is the sound of knife
What is the sound of rock
What is the sound of bone
        of knife on bone on rock
What is the sound of crazy
What is the sound of sex
        of sex on crazy on knife and bone
What is the sound of hair snapping
What is the sound of hair matting
What is the sound of a single hair on a map of bone
        of a lap of teeth snapping
What is the sound of a weapon of flesh
What is the sound of a muted face
        of muted eyes made mute in a stare of scream

What becomes of the sound
one hand makes as it beats itself to death

What Is This Place?

Not in afterlife
or in nature—
but in

Beirut, Sidon, Kabul, Gaza
Soweto, Lima, Santiago, Jerusalem
Managua, New York, Little Rock, Chicago
El Salvador, Khartoum, Berlin
Pine Ridge, Seoul, Atlanta, Belfast
Londonderry, Riga, Tunis, Addis Abbaba
Minsk, Vitebsk, Bucharest
Los Angeles, Nablus, Teheran, Lhasa
Caracas, Calcutta, Vienna, Columbo

rubble of war: class, race, religion—
temples of hatred and fear.
Hell is a human invention.

Annunciation

for Hideo Hashimoto
March 25, 1984

On Columbus Day, 1962,
the man stands in the Peace
Garden in Hiroshima—
his dead nephew appears,
a ravaged child of twelve,
tells him his home across
the sea has been swallowed
by a typhoon, tells him
the sign, "This will never
happen again," is a lie:

tells him of Vietnam
and Cambodia eaten as by
white devils from Manchuria,
tells him of future assassins,
Nicaragua's agony and
civil war in El Salvador—
tells him of an American president's
boast of one million bombs like that
of Hiroshima—
tells him of an incident—
  then the boy stops
    unable to say what he sees
    as if he had been killed
  by yet another bright light
and then the dead boys says

"The destiny of humankind
is in your hands.
I am destroyed but
you can still help.
Go and tell them
I said this—
open your hands
and reach across lands
to lay down arms
and play the music
of life with your kin,
with your future."

And then the boy disappeared,
and what remained was
the distant sound of a whale,
barely singing, and alone
on the Earth.

August Sixth, Noon, Fortieth Anniversary

Little Boy dropped
from deathship
named Enola Gay
for the bombadier's mother—
Little Boy drowned
in the body of the city
he raped.

Headlines today:
President of the United States
describes cancerous pimple
removed from his nose,
caused by seventy years
of Hollywood sun—
side by side
with a small paragraph
on Seiko Ikeda,
Hiroshima victim
who, one August morning
when she was twelve,
woke up with no face.

Lamentation

One day in spring
a donkey in Israel
was decorated with flags:
on one side Palestine's
on the other side Israel's.
Someone shot the donkey.
It doesn't matter which side.

A widow and mother of three
was killed during a bus
hijacking on her way
to work at a nuclear plant
in the desert.
Soldiers and terrorists
(all of them trembling).
Someone's gun caught her.
It doesn't matter whose.

Olive trees were uprooted
from home and stolen
for decoration downtown
across the Green Line.
Arabs and Jews replanted
small seedlings together.
Then these were uprooted.

How long will human-
kind tear open its heart
to beat out the other side
at history?

Peace Dragon of Hiroshima (48″ × 36″) Acrylic enamel on aluminum. 1976.

This painting (one of seven) is in the permanent collection at the Peace Memorial Park in Hiroshima, Japan. The work portrays a mythologic dragon dropping lotus blossoms (an Oriental symbol of everlasting life) on the bombed-out shell of the city of Hiroshima. As a mother of five children, I have lived all my life with the world at war or threatened by war. My thoughts and prayers have always been for the safety of my own children and grandchildren and for the safety of all mothers' children throughout the world. While I realize that the power of the first atomic bomb needed to be made known to end the Pacific War, the manner in which it was demonstrated seems especially barbaric. It was dropped on a civilian population at 8:15 in the morning when all the gas jets from breakfast cooking were on, and the streets were filled with little children enroute to school. When I visited Hiroshima in 1976, I was profoundly touched by the tragedy of that nuclear event and the suffering it brought to the children. Upon returning to the United States, I painted my prayer for world peace and a feeling of love and reconciliation for the Japanese people.

"As the Bomb Fell, We Saw
Blue Lightning"

Blue lightning flashes.
Fireclouds fly down the mountain.
Under the full moon the Earth
awaits her devastation.

Softly here a spring storm
darkens morning, a spring snow
covers all. In the thick light
comes the explosion.

Yet we still can breathe.
Our skin gives forth
no blue smoke, our eyes
do not yet see the utter

nothing black
of a heavy
rain of
ash.

Death of the Fertile Earth Goddess: Strip Mining
(69″ × 60″) Oil on canvas. 1976.

This painting depicts the crucifixion of the soil as practiced by coal companies strip mining in Wyoming, and my outrage at the resulting destruction of the soil fertility. Animal skulls, bleaching on western telephone poles and fence posts, are a common sight in western United States. They put the viewer in mind of crucifixion scenes.

Transfiguration

*Given to the permanent collection
of the Peace Memorial Garden, Hiroshima,
August 6, 1980.*

Children of Earth, where are You?

How important it is to forget.
How important it is to forget.
How important it is to remember.

I

Not so long ago and already
we have forgotten, only a little
longer than one young lifetime,
only a little more than last year,
only a few minutes ago and we
have forgotten, forgotten.

It is time, children, it is time.

Let me speak, say the mothers
Let me speak, say the grandmothers
Let me speak, say the fathers and brothers
Hear me! cry the sisters and daughters

From the past and from the future
the hands of the dead are beating
upward on the Earth for our attention.

We will live, say the flowers
We will live, say the trees
We will live, cry the rivers
We will live, roar the oceans
We will live, sing the children

No more acid in our rains
No more firewind in our brains
No more stars shot from the sky
  to kill us a thousand times
No more blindness to hide the terrible
  brilliance of so many faces
  exploding like stars
  all over the world
No more lack of thought for the unborn
No more lack of love for the living

2

See them, the mollusk mothers,
crouching from the sea,
their soft bodies the saviors
of our pain, those who went before

come forth from their shells
to show us their wounds
no sea sponge can heal.
Only our vision is their hope.
Only their eyes can show us the truth.

Come gather the pearls,
our mothers' eyes set free in time,
their bones and flesh a fine powder
crushed and turned into foam,
turned into light, light,
the power of light leaping
forever against the dark pride
of Hades, giant shark of the West,
his teeth held at bay by only
the light of their glistening,
the light of their transforming pain.
Come gather the pearls in your arms
and listen and see.

See the mollusk mothers rising
from the wounds of the past
to give us our future:

        Remember
          Remember

3

Children of Earth,
eat no more the food of death
but return to the land of the living.

Now let lotuses lift their leaves
through the circle of your arms.

Come, make loving covenant
with us, a promise

To cherish
To protect
To rise eternally
        from the broken light
        from the muddied, bloodied waters
        from the unnatural fires of history

To reach hands across this sea
and make the kiss of peace
blot out your mothers' tears.

Peace Tree (41″ × 51″) Oil on canvas. 1989.

A Blessing to Be

Here no human hand bends
against my grain,
no human voice chimes
out of tune with mine—
frog and jaybird,
swallow and hawk
make music with my time.

Here no telephone drains
my spirit with demands,
no mail calls forth my name—
cricket and deer combine
to keep my spirit sane.

Here no hysteric cry
wakens with my day,
no thwarting of the soul
consumes my right to play.

No tragic triangulation,
no blame or shame of soul
peculiar to my kind,
no anti-creative neurosis
invented by civilized minds
imposes itself on my world.
Only the bee and the moth
intrude and surprise,
curious and friendly,
the grasshopper leaps
at my feet as I rise up
in praise.

I never tire of loving
my valley or being
loved by its trees.
Eros agrees, giving
health to my being
while I smooch with the iris
and dance with the breeze.

On occasion, I seek
company with my own kind,
but I have lived too long
in the wonder of others
to be self-satisfied
with just my own species.

*I portray the Peace Tree (from Black Elk's
vision of a blossoming tree of peace) with its
roots growing out of old, disused weapons of
war. The tree has four sturdy branches,
representing the four races of humans—red,
yellow, black and white. These four colors of
humanity are depicted by the figures within
the circle in the tree trunk.*

*I dedicate this painting to the wives and
mothers everywhere, most especially to those
in the Russian city of Stavropal, who publicly
protested (January 1990) the calling up of
their sons and husbands into active duty. They
shouted furiously, "I won't give up my son.
We put up with everything. We put up with
it! How long are we going to put up with
everything?" Because of this powerful protest
from mothers, Russian leaders abandoned
the calling up of army reserves.*

Country Cousins

Sing, Cousin Swallow,
Growl, Cousin Bear—

Go on about your being,
Wee Cousin Frog.

I want to open
the heart
of my ear
to your sound,
open my heart
to your song.

　　Soorooo, Cousin Owl,
　　Floorooo, Cousin Fish,
　　Oohooo, Cousin Loon,
　　ShooShooo, Cousin Moth,
　　To you, Cousin Human.

　　And the silence
　　of the Tree
　　and the stillness
　　of the Sky
　　and the Sound
　　that They make
　　when They meet.

Protecting, Celebrating and Loving the Earth and Her Children

In this section we find some of the pieces upon which we build hope, support, strength and community. Women who practice women's spirituality know that it is essential to be awe-filled with wonder and grandeur at the bounty and blessings of Gaia, our Earth. Many of us know that taking time out, to be in and at one with nature is to be re-energized. A camping trip, praying on a mountain top, receiving the spray of a waterfall, watching an otter swim across a lake, soaking in a sunset, fresh flowers on a kitchen table, walking through a botanical garden or a woods, petting a cat or holding a small child, being present at the wondrous moments of life-force transformation in the forms of birth and death—all these and more, renew our sense of mystery and joy in life. The Goddess is life-based, creation-centered, the celebration of life-force. In an age of nuclear warfare and power, in a technological age, we must re-connect with, remember our mother Earth and our own bodies. Earth-based, nature-centered religions can help us to do this.

We also find hope in community—in acting in solidarity with others involved in social action, peace and justice, ecological renewal movements—and in personal growth, holistic health, in the Twelve Steps of Alcoholics Anonymous, Al-Anon and other recovery programs.

Red Road to the Dome House (24″ × 36″) Oil on canvas.
1983.

*My love of the South Dakota Black Hills
is pictured here by the use of hyped-up
emotional coloration. The painting describes
my scarcely contained excitement as I travel
the red clay road leading to the Barkley Art
Center studio.*

Hymn to Gaea

Mother Earth's sweet green fur,
or sun-bleached bones of sand
or red-parched skin of shale,
the children swimming in her blood—
marvelous manatee in gentle hospitality
or shy-singing whale,
coral, starfish and eel,
seahorse, plankton and pearl,
and land angels of elk,
eland, ibex and deer,
giraffe and lion and the beautiful bear,
foxglove, human child, and wonderful wolf,
and into infinity of stars I sing,
and I sing of them all, enthralled,
enraptured in you, Beloved One,
in all your creation,
every molecule a miracle!

Mazama

To see what the Mountain sees
you climb the Creature.
I watch below, content to see
the Mountain.

But you move and make
the ascent to become one
with the Mountain, to marry Her.

No longer I and Thou
you and She are
a vertical We
or one white being, all I.

You become ice and fire,
cloud-bearer, light-breather.
You become Her body's lover,
human past human,
as those who can fly—
you become true child of the Sky.

Mazama: The primordial mountain whose cataclysmic eruption six thousands years ago formed Oregon's Crater Lake, deepest body of water on the continent, a still-living volcanic caldera.

Chamberlain, South Dakota, marks the meeting of the eastern prairie country and the western rolling hills and mountains. This landscape, painted in arbitrary, assigned colors reflects my anticipatory excitement on leaving the flat lands and the Missouri River valley as the climb toward the Black Hills and my summer studio begins. In this painting I am singing the praises of the awesome spaces of the South Dakota landscape.

Road Out of Chamberlain (24″ ×36″) Oil on canvas, 1983.

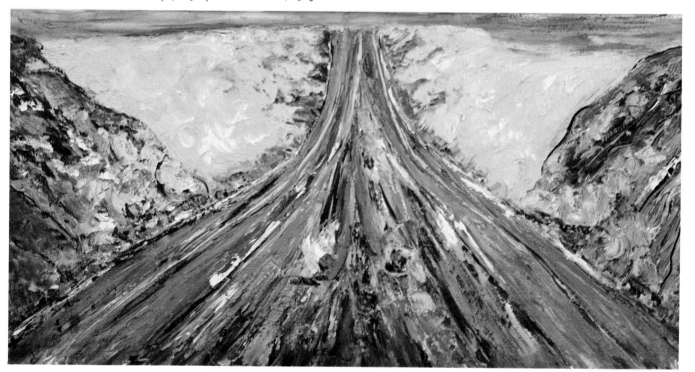

Red Tree in Landscape (18″ × 24″) Oil on canvas. 1983.

The assigned, hyped colors of this Black Hills landscape parallel my intense wonderment of the land and tree forms that encircle my summer studio.

Five Trees

I should like to
make my life's work
a gift of myself
to one tree.

Once I saw a tree
in Illinois.
Hypnotized by a
dull professor
into an altered
state, just
then I looked
out the window.
It was March
and the tree
was still
naked, magnificient.
I awakened too quickly
to remember its name,
but it had twelve arms
and thirteen elbows
and a bass oboe voice.

There are four trees
around my house.
Their invisible arms
reach out to protect
with a circle. I am
grateful and glad.

Meanwhile, though
I know their anthropoetic names:
crab, maple, red maple, silver birch,
it will take me forty years
to really see each tree
and four hundred more to learn
the name each one calls itself.
By then we shall all
be changed anyway.

Schooled by the cardinal
and cedar waxwing
in the backyard
I have at least
figured this much out.

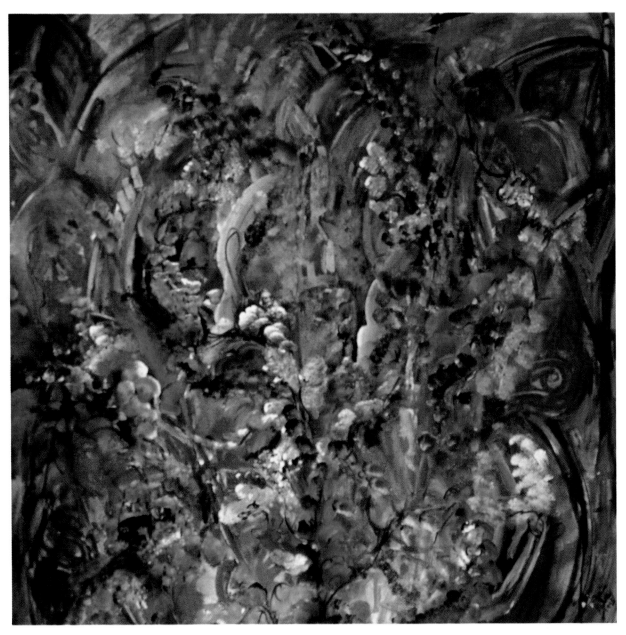

Magic Garden (65″ × 65½″) Oil on canvas. 1974.

Being an exuberant gardener, I am fantasizing in this painting of a flower garden bursting with energy, color, and form. My magical garden on canvas never needs to be weeded, hoed or watered and blooms profusely.

My Feet Press Flowers

My feet press flowers
back into Earth, unseen
fragility, roots too small
for the fertile eye.

Sweet green breath of trees
and grasses gives sensual
life to me;
under night cover our breaths
chemically conform.

For breakfast, tree eats
my skinned off cells
from Earth, I eat
the fruit of the tree,
give thanks for life
deliciously

on our preciously edible planet.

All Kinds of Risings

There are all kinds of risings:

the rising of daffodils,
of hungry lover's lips,
of breasts to the kiss,
of pressed down people
to their own dignity,
of old fear and lost love.

We hear about these indirectly,
after, and the difficulty
the witnesses had being believed.

Telling the story over and over
begging to be believed, longing
to belong, yearning for
faithful ears.

Do not be overcome
by despair.
Continue, even though
others lack a certain

imagination.
Spend one month
practicing
the impossible.
Being happy
is a skill.

To befriend the body
and its pain is to move
beyond death toward
original joy.

Remember your own
and the other's
Mystery.

I AM

You are

   I   mmortal

   A   stonishing

   M   ore

You have no need for a name—
   You are.
But we need to know You,
we need to be able to call on You,
greet You, invite You, entreat You,
wish You Good Morning and
thank You for a good day and
all the stars.

      And so we ask
      Who are You?
      meaning, What
      is Your name?

The only time You spoke
You spoke in fire.
Did the prophet hear
crackles of Your laughter
coming out of the glowing
green boughs?
"I have no name but
you want to call Me
something, Friend, and
I agree.
You cannot call Me No Name,
so call Me what—I Am.
      Essence of flame
      Breath of sky
      Being of light
      Sound of the dark
        I Am

And remember, Beloved,
      You are
My image.
To give Me worth and praise
you must simply be yourself,
claiming all complexity and
infinitude, for you are
      I Am.
We are relatives,
Essence and essence,
Mystery and mystery,

      We are."

Tribal Traditions

When women began to meet together and create alternative celebrations, most of us started by modifying the liturgies, worship services or rituals of our religious traditions. Early, we were concerned that these celebrations be more participatory, less hierarchal, more Earth centered. Some of us began to reclaim more ancient celebrations like the New Moon rituals of Jewish tradition. Artists among us began to add music, chants and altars. We celebrated seasons, moon phases, life transitions. We created baby blessings, house blessings, rituals to honor anger and rage, and rituals of healing.

At some point, those of us who were researching women's history began to realize that we had found in our collective unconscious the remnants of ancient Earth-centered nature traditions, including Wicca, Native American and African spirituality, and that of indigenous tribal peoples throughout the globe. We began to actively research and validate these traditions.

Wicca, often called the Old Religion, is a nature-based tradition that celebrates the seasons and cycles of life. It pays great attention to plant and crop lore and animal spirits and knowledge. There is no dogma, sacred revealed truth or central authority. From the study of Wicca we have re-membered ancient European traditions that honor the Earth, the goddess, women's bodies and the arts of ritual.

From African traditions we learned ancestral veneration and to acknowledge spiritual connections with the past. We learned to value the powers of rhythm, dance, music and creativity as a means of survival.

Native American and other mystical traditions have taught us the themes that scientists are just now beginning to prove. We are all of one substance, the Earth, the waters, the rocks, the plants, the four-legged, winged, and two-legged ones. We are interconnected and dependent on one another. The blessing of the Lakota Sioux is "Aho Mitakuye Oyasin," ("To all my relatives"). They raise prayer flags in four colors—red, yellow, black and white—to honor the four colors of humans, the four directions and the four elements—earth, air, fire and water.

Selu: Corn Fertility Goddess (24″ × 30″) Oil on canvas. 1988-89.

Livey

"She walks in the rain as if it is sun."

Alice Walker, of her daughter,
in *Living by the Word*

Her hair is the first thing
I think of about her—I want
to say "remember" but I never
knew her except through stories
told by my Grandma, her
granddaughter-in-law:
She could *stand* on her hair,
and braided it into natural waves.
Hair being the pure power
of unmitigated self-acceptance,
and of playful sensuous delight.
I re-member her hair.

The next thing is how
she taught herself to read and write
in foreign languages: English and French.
She was Osage, Iroquois Nation,
and of royal descent.
Of all my ancestors, she is the noblest
—except for my Russian peasant
Mama with aristocrat's blood.
They both married soldiers.
Mama's soldier was a prince
in restaurant-owner's clothing.
He smelled of cabbage borsht
until she took him to California
where his heart gave out and died.
Livey's soldier was a Confederate
in the unCivil War before
the United States.
Which is the third thing
I know about her:

She fetched for him
when he'd demand her
presence from another room
to throw a log on the fire
not two feet from his.

Then—and I'm not sure
if this is fantasy or legend
—she broke away one day
without so much as a
"Do it yourself, Old Man."
Just off she went,
a self-taught teacher,
proud in her body
and brave-minded,
unafraid to use
her strength and skill.

And after that the legend dims,
the story grows silent,
and I, alone, imagine:
She went to the edge
of her world and grew wings.

O, Livey, great-great-
grandmother of mine,
when I demand of myself
the impossible and make it,
it's you in my blood.
And that I know for a fact.
And wherever else you are,
I thank you.

Grandmother Corn brought corn out of her earth-womb for the people. This painting abounds with fertility symbols. The life-giving, pregnant woman is surrounded by growing corn, dragonflies dropping their eggs, the moon—symbol of woman's cyclical fertility—in her headdress, and the meander pattern of her skirt is a metaphor for life-giving river water. The association of female images with meanders was found in western Romania in 5000 B.C.E. as the goddess Vodastra. It is also found in the Neolithic, Copper, and Iron Ages as well as in the artifacts of the Anasazi Indians of North America.

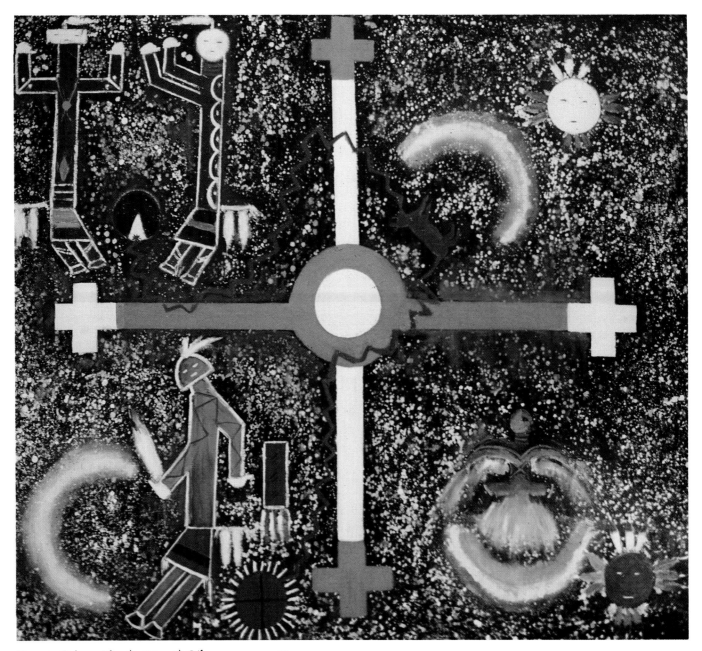

Coyote Brings Fire (82" × 70") Oil on canvas. 1988.

American Indian mythology explains how humans received the gift of fire stolen from the campfire of the gods of heaven. A sly coyote then wandered through the heavenly bodies carrying the fire and passing the sun, the moon, and the stars. He then brought the fire to the tipi of first man and first woman.

Coyote

Rough road trails
through Crazy Mountains
into the Bear Tooth Range.
I am Autumn.
We follow the river
east, to greet the dawn-sun.

Beside the road, your body,
Old Coyote, Trickster,
miracle-giver, birth-bestower,
time-keeper. A truck hit you hard.

Your spirit rose up, laughing,
howling with laughter.
I see patches of your calico fur
where your children buried you
in their mouths.
I see teethmarks on your long
and delicately pointed ears.
I see amber blaze on desert oak trees.
I see green turning to blood on leaves.
I see with your dark stone eyes, Coyote.
Everywhere, I see where your spirit went.

Red Lizards in Red Landscape (24″ × 30″) Oil on canvas.
1989.

This painting is of a dream landscape stained passion-red, orange and pink and inhabited by dream lizards.

Has Anyone Ever Died of Bad Dreams?

All night lizards
eat away the shell
around my mind

letting old lovers in
old pains resume
a tiresome rhythm

I hear helpless cries
occasionally, unable
to discern words

but a relentless plea—
Wake me! Wake me!
This dream harms me!
No well-wishing here.

Emptying countless
wastebaskets, relining them
with fresh newspapers

stripping, washing,
changing sheets,
arranging flowers

ceaselessly. What mockery
to call this rest,
the mind an amoeba
dividing itself under cover
of night, the sleeper mother
to the Self or Self the mad

mother to the dream.
I nurse my wounds into morning,
struggle to birth me awake,

find a new face
rippled in the mirror
covered with the scars of sleep.

Eagles Holding up the Night Sky (60″ × 216″) Oil on canvas. 1987-88.

Cosmic Circus

I am animalspirit,
animate, I leap,
I dive, I breathe,
I die, I always return.

As long as the universe
lives, I belong.

Cosmic Child

Worldflesh—my bones
bones of the old
Red Stars.

Humans have created fantasies about the night sky from the beginning of time. In this painting, I combine the contemporary Cambridge Atlas of Astronomy *tracking of our solar system with an ancient American Indian myth that contends that bats, eagles and the souls of departed Indians are holding up the night sky.*

Braids

Mother Nature weaves a veil
with starsilken threads:
methane, ammonia, nitrogen
mists for mystic allure
of interplanetary magnetism.

Moon, Moon, O cratered Moon,
tossed like a beloved ball
between your parent Jupiter
and big sister Ganymede,
little Io, all-red volcano,
your hot liquid heart constantly
opening itself to the sky!

Then why not let Saturn defy
further laws and braid
her daughter rings around her,
a golden cord of fire and light
to welcome eternal night,
the yellow wings of morning?

The Elements Are in Charge

We live in
a place where
only the elements
are really
in charge,

and we are
all subject
to change,
and

the truth is,
we are in need
of comfort.

Vulture Mother: The Bird Goddess in her Vulture Aspect
(70″ × 58″) Oil on canvas. 1988.

The dark bird of the dead is welcoming all creatures back to the earth-womb from where we all come and to where we all return. The double triangle is a symbol of the goddess. Both life and death symbols abound in this painting. The sky contains both vulture birds and fertile dragon flies. There is a rainbow of hope around the head of the goddess. Life and death are intertwined.

Eskimo Crone

"Old woman, why do I fear you?"
"Child, you are afraid you will
catch my death."

Imagine

Imagine
place and body
so in harmony
you take off
your clothes

Imagine
place and soul
so in harmony
you take off
your body.

Imminence

Long time overdue, past time—
friends come to sit with me
like many fathers, yet I am
the one who paces, paces.
Watch me tear curtains
and chew the door jamb,
watch me strangle furniture,
eat wood.

This birth I await is death.

Watch the house grow thin around me
as I fill with the weight of time.
Watch me sleep between the greater pains
and dream the dream I cannot let go.
No surrender, I hold the future
here in my womb, no dread. Am willing
to pass only this present terror.

The death I await is birth.

Sacrificial Trees (30″ × 48″) Oil on canvas. 1989.

This is a comparative religious painting. Christ, of Christian theology, sacrificed himself on a tree (the cross) for the salvation of humankind. The Plains Indians offered their pain and suffering for the good of the tribe in their sun dance ritual. Attached to a sacred cottonwood tree by leather thongs or ropes through slits in their chest muscles, they sacrifice their blood so that the people might live. Compassionate women bear witness to both sacrifices. The anguish of Mary witnessing the death of her son on the cross and the Indian mothers' torment for their sons' torturous ordeal is one of the most agonizing of all emotions.

Sacrificial Trees

"When I pray, I pray
in Lakota and English.
Our people need to hear
there is truth in both.
I'm a Lakota.
I'm a Christian.
I pray to one God."
         The Rev. Virgil Foote

In a circle of suns
gathering powers
we pray in four directions,
we pray the four colors,
the races,
we blow the eagle breast-
whistle between teeth
when bone becomes
weakened in pain;
we fly the four winds
with our feet in time
with Earthmother heart-
drumming her cry—

prayer ties fly
in all colors,
driven by need
to this. Tree-circled
we pray for the world.

For world wounds to heal.
Wounds between the colors,
between races, between men
and women, between parents
and children, between all
animals and our species,
between us and the trees.

This sacred tree, the cottonwood,
prayed into for a year, preparing,
partakes of the sacrifice.
O Tree, become a bond,
be to us a Binding Back Tree
to Earthmother and God,
a focus for our need to be One.
Uprooted as we, you share our grief,
you carry our prayer, you bear
our blood as in agony we pull away
from you.

May this blood be to you a gift,
communion gift, and help us
O Binding Tree! Help us
with your ancient knowing,
wisdom of four elements,
creation encircled.

May our tears be your water,
our drumming your safe fire,
your blooming our earth
and your leaving our breath.

Another tree cut down
and cruciform carries a Christ
sacrificed also, all blood
gone out, that corpse
becomes our Spring.

See, new budding-forth blossoms
from green-gashed eyes.
No one dares look into them.

White Buffalo Woman, remember!
We are your body's children!
Madonna of Mercy, hear!

As sun rises and sets we pray,
may your tears of compassion
rain on our dry season of fear!

Between the bare and bearing trees
the Woman sits serene,
She Who Holds Peace in her hands,
the sacred pipe whose power is:
Be reconciled. Be still. Behold.

At the skirt of the danced out tree
she waits, watches, prays.
Her birthdance incomplete,
her blood shall flow
into life again.

Sagecrown, protect her.
Mother of the Year chosen well.
Compassion. Compassion between
the brow-sweat and the blood of your son.
Compassion between the Earth and the Tree.
Compassionate skin-gift from your opening
arms. Dancing Compassion.

You sit on the ground,
well-grounded,
at one.

Outsider, mother of yearning,
you become Heart of the Circle of Mystery,
a living stone in the sacred dance,
a place of peace.

You are the altar
on which their sacrificial
drama is offered and made.

Healed in the worldwomb of Time
may we be.

Brave and still
may we be.

Respectful and one may we know
ourselves as daughters and sons
of One Mother, One God.

May this Dance be fulfilled,
this Heartcry be sung
out of death into life.
And neither in vain.

Celebration

Not within alone,
not without alone,
not either/or,
here or there,
but both
within, without,
and all.

The divinely Loving One
lives within you, radiant
in the temple of your heart,
resting at your inner hearth,
your body's core, and the fire
that flows through your vessels
is divine, and all your vessels
holy, and your openings and closings
also holy.

And the warmth created in your blood
is the same warmth as the golden sun
gives forth, flooding Earth with light and life.
And so the stars are temples also, and all
rivers and seas and tiny, invisible animals
and every plant and tree, also a temple.

And the Loving One wakes and moves,
dreams and dances in the spaces
around each atom, and flies the electric
hoops that give each one its name.

And in each atom's center is
the Holy One's bed, and also beyond.

We—you and I and stars and seas—are
fruit of the Holy One's passion,
our limbs and laughter, light and air
and our darkness, ice and fire—all
longed and loved into being by God's deep desire.

Within you, within me, lies a godling seed,
fed by our love toward its birthing.
And in that emerging will be great gentleness
and grace—pleasure and yearning delight,
and Creator/Creation in full-filling embrace.

For God is Both and All,
within and beyond,
O! Most Intimate Mystery!
In you and in me,
in the rock and the tree,
and in all the spaces
between.

Spirituality and the New Sciences

Science, philosophy, art and religion have often dealt with the same metaphysical issues—How did the world begin? How did human life come into being? What happens after death? In our time and culture, these disciplines often have been separated. Today this is beginning to change. Many of us are making connections between ancient earth-based traditions, goddess history and images, feminist philosophies, contemporary needs of humans and of our planet Earth, and the new sciences, including quantum physics and the Gaia Theory. The themes in this book are dependent on developments in the sciences of archeology, anthropology, biology, geology, feminist psychology, and new methods of academic scholarship. In a time of transition, we can look both to our past and to the future to find possible options to build new life-supporting values.

Feminists are not the only ones aware of this "spirit." Physicists speak in terms of simultaneity and synchronicity. We do not think, act or create in isolation. We are connected, even physically, in ways that our poets, mystics and tribal traditions have taught us, ways that scientists are just beginning to name.

Some theologians are telling us that we have been without a cosmology, or creation story, for three hundred years—since the split between science and organized religion. They speak of our need to reconnect our knowledge of our physical world with our myth systems and our religious ethical stories.

Scientists say that Energy is constant, it cannot be created or destroyed, only transformed. Therefore, each of us was present at the moment of the creation of our universe. Priest and poet Alla Bozarth says, "There are Stars in our Bones." Native American peoples pray a blessing to honor the Earth, the rocks, the trees, the waters, the creatures, the humans. They say, "We are all related." We are all as one with the universe.

Perhaps one of the most important lessons of the 21st century is that the age of individualism is dead, that what each one of us thinks and does affects all the rest of us. Women have had a great awareness of relationships, family and community that we can bring to address global concerns. This does not mean there is no room for great multiplicity and diversity; it does mean we must begin to be much more humble about our "one right answer."

Dance of Shakti, Creator of the Universe: The 11½ Million Mile High Dancer (69″ × 84″) Oil on canvas. 1989.

Cosmic Birth Dance

I am
woman, life-changer,
cosmic creator.
My skin I wear and shed
like a worn-out clothing,
falls away, falls away
cell by cell now.

I have come
to climax
and turn
toward new
creation,
bliss-bound
to new life-nurture.
All within,
bliss-bound, I nurture.

I have no green,
but dream I dance
in tongues of fire,
Shakti to Shiva,
and one with the round
of death and life
that is
creation, I also
sing an everlasting
night into morning.

I walk once more
your forests, quake
through your secret
deserts exposing all,
illumining all. . . .

I come to teach
and heal in a word
of love.
I come! I come!
Earth, make room!

The dance and desire
are one
who
  becoming fire
    most becoming
      be coming, sing, singe, surge, soar—!

I am
feminine God
emerging
in light Light!   LIGHT

Breathe Me—
I AM — LIFE — Am FLAME

In this work, Shakti (female) represents the embodiment of wisdom, intelligence, creative power and the birthing of the universe. Hers is a dance of endless cosmic energy—that of both creation and destruction that involves the whole of the universe. The atoms (DNA) which she flings into space are the same as those found in our galaxy and in our human bodies. When we are returned to the earth in death, and, later, when our earth may die or explode or reform in the ensuing eons of time, we shall be a part of some future star, perhaps. We are made of the stuff of stars—there are stars in our bones. As stars, we will eventually return to the eternity of the great cyclical process.

Creation

In the beginning
hydrogen.
And then
the Explosion.

We, the fragments
tumbling to Infinity,
part of the One
expanding the Origins,
born out of the Chaos of God.

"Cosmic Birth Dance" is a composite of the following poems: "Virgin Birth," "Oracle," "Morning Bouquet," and "Tantra Poem."

Creation of the Universe: Primal Energy Burst
(60″ × 61″) Oil on canvas. 1975.

In this painting, I portray the primal source energy (DNA). Any part of the cosmos would have been indistinguishable from any other part. The resulting common, interacting energies are shared by the whole of the universe: stars, moons, suns, planets, plants, animals, insects, birds, humans. This work reflects my philosophy of the interrelatedness of all things and lays to rest any illusion of an isolated ego. Everything is connected and related to all that is. There is a basic oneness in the universe, and all events and all things are so interrelated that in each one is found all others.

Sunday Memory

Something like the speed of light
—your image in my Sunday bright
doorway, a memory.

In the living room in your arms
I remembered everything for an instant—
remembered, whether again or before,
that I have loved you always,
remembered the goodness we are,
remembered the mystery of your face
and my smile in your oceanblue eyes,
remembered the precise angle of your kiss,
how your hand fit over my breast, exactly,

  and that somewhere
  we have traded blood
  and become one heart.

We have belonged to light,
and slowed to these particular bodies,
and shall return to light again.
And when we do, shall we remember then
that we have been these bodies, embracing
in sunlight in pure joy, and
that we have loved each other?

Family Reunion

Six million years since
Grandma and Grandpa Bacteria
hatched up the possibility
of the rest of us.

Now chestnut, sandpiper, turtle,
eagle, human, lily, mushroom
and horse have climbed out
of the crack in our cosmic egg,
riding the Great Light.

We are more complicated,
to be sure, more long-lived,
more opinionated and fragile—
but not more creative,
extravagant, or efficient
than our great-grandparents,
those one-celled creatures
that still live in our midst,
that still have the power
to give us life
and also to kill,

to whom we owe
our power to breathe
and birth and laugh,
write plays, wage sports,
learn peace, or kill
ourselves.

Chrysalis

   I find myself
   in the time between selves.
      Transition

I am pregnant with myself.
Do you realize what this means?
It means that every part of me must die,
all my cells and organs open and dissolve,
for I need their juicy substances
to nurture my new blood:
let teeth become eyes,
gullet become brain,
grey become bright red,
and hair turn into wings.
This is the truth of me—
I was, am, and shall be
 my Self, forever new,
  forever changed by changing,
creature blessed by consciousness,
 alive.

And this is not
a voiceless act, but a process
resounding inside death
with lusty shouts and whoops,
irregular and visible below
the carcass veil.
And death grows thinner,
giving way to God-knows-What—
diminishing like gauze
of spun sugar melting in the sun.

Soon, I will be full-ripe
with my Self,
able to nurse on sweet nectar,
free and light as living rain.
Soon, I will fly.

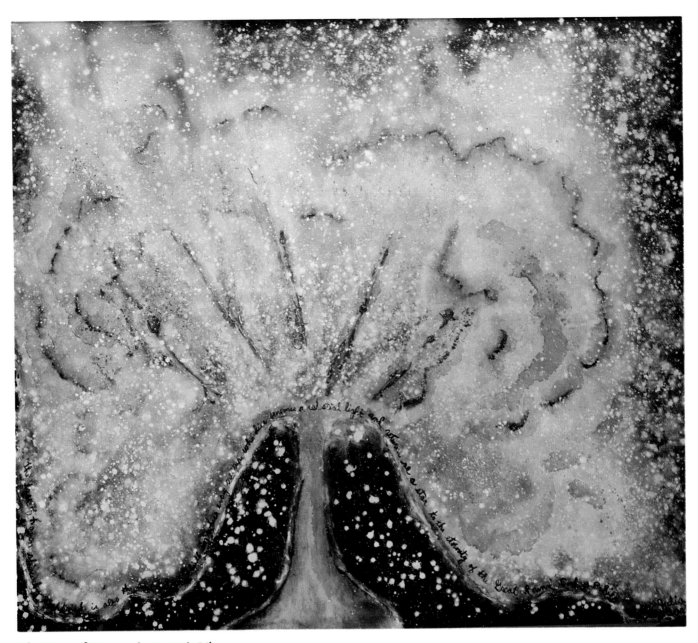

The Tree of Heaven (70″ × 60″) Oil on canvas. 1977.

"The tree of heaven shines by night and is the soul tree of re-birth in which every creature who dies becomes a celestial light and returns as a star to the eternity of the Great Round."   Book of Bahir

Night sky viewed as a huge tree where departed souls shine as stars in mystic lore. Modern physics now recognizes this truth by telling us that over the millenia we evolved from the stuff of stars and will return again to the eternity of the Great Round when our Earth eventually disintergrates and then reforms as a new star. The cosmic energy dance goes on in endless motion.

Biodance

everything bears the property of Love

Sitting on a rock in the Salmon River
watching first leaves fall.

From sunhigh mountain treetops
upstream the rapids carry
old branches to the sea,
their leaves landlocked already.

Why so soon?
Not soon at all—
your time is complete.
And so is mine.

You rest in sunlight
before transforming
into earth and air.

You dissolve your leafy form
and recompose into a thousand bodies.

Nothing ever ends.
Everything is always
    beginning.

Shall I find myself tomorrow
shining in a waterdrop
on a piece of moss
on the bark of a tree
that once was you?

Green into burntred,
old leaf, our biodance began
millenia ago, but today
I am glad to see you clearly
for the first time
with just these eyes,
my changing
partner!

Your bronze body
turns to powder
with a crack
beneath my foot.

Part of you has already become me.
You are on your new way.

You will be back.
And so will I.
    So will I.

Belonging

The small plot of ground
on which you were born
cannot be expected

to stay forever
the same.
Earth changes,
and home
becomes different
places.

You took flesh
from clay
but the clay
did not come
from just one
place.

To feel alive,
important, and safe,
know your own waters
and hills, but know
more.

You have stars
in your bones
and oceans
in blood.

You have opposing
terrain in each eye.

You belong to the land
and sky of your first cry,
you belong to infinity.

Creature Covenant

"And if the Chain of Being goes on, and we are only
the end of it because we are blind to anything that is
beyond us, then perhaps Plato's Intelligible Realms are
filled with those creatures of pure Mind and Music that
used to be called angels. . . . Above us in the food chain
may be angels, below us may be goblins and fairies."

Imaginary Landscape, William Irwin Thompson

To W.I.T.:

Deep in the anaerobic dark
of my gut, is it fairies
I have eaten, now
having a blast, going out
with a war cry to announce
themselves?

In Fairy Faith, these
ancient wise ones
will let their presence
be known no matter
the form—onion, fungi,
or nut.

Though they be sandwiched
between poetry and cybernetic
truths, their mutable powers
live on and become me.

In innocence I have
devoured my elders,
gobbled goblins,
their wrathful cousins
who shriek gracelessly
at having yielded their world
to us.

I beg their pardon,
make a pact, enter
creature covenant
with those I have eaten:
in me and my deeds,
may your dreams be fulfilled.

If I prove worthy and true
one day in my turn
I may be angel food.

Index of Poems

Alla Renée Bozarth

Alla Bozarth is the daughter of an artistic Russian immigrant mother and an Episcopal priest father. Her mother painted; her father wrote poetry. Both were dramatic performers. As an only child, Alla absorbed the artistic and spiritual gifts of her parents as her legacy. She traces her vocation as a spiritual midwife symbolically to her great-grandmother, a teacher and midwife, and to her mother who worked through Church World Service to help displaced persons find new homes. Her passion for the sensual and meaningful word comes from her paternal grandmother, with whom much of her solitary childhood was spent in the shared enjoyment of literature—from Shakespeare and the Psalms to Allen Ginsberg and Emily Dickinson. Alla draws inspiration from her Osage Indian great-great-grandmother, who was a self-taught linguist. During her academic years in theology and the performing arts at Northwestern University, Alla received an urban education, marching to Peoria in the Hunger Caravan with Jesse Jackson and experiencing the powerful emotions of the peace and justice movements of the early seventies. Later she married her seminary colleague and moved from Chicago to Minneapolis, Minnesota, where she developed Wisdom House, a feminist healing and worshiping community. Alla's marriage of fourteen years was creatively rich, as she shared dance and music in ministry with her Episcopal priest husband, a profoundly gifted singer. After his sudden death in 1985, Alla returned to her earth-roots at the foot of Mt. Hood in western Oregon, where her priestly ministry continues, and she experiences healing and growth "through the mystery of being alone—all one—" in the presence of her "personal power spots—the sacred mountain and the gypsy ocean" of the Oregon coast.

BOOKS:
At the Foot of the Mountain, CompCare, 1990.
A Journey Through Grief, CompCare, 1990.
Womanpriest: A Personal Odyssey, rev. ed., Luramedia, 1988.
Love's Prism, Sheed and Ward, 1987.
Life Is Goodbye/Life Is Hello, rev. ed., CompCare, 1986.
Sparrow Songs, Wisdom House, 1982.
The Word's Body, The University of Alabama Press, 1979.
Gynergy, Wisdom House, 1978.
In the Name of the Bee & the Bear & the Butterfly, Wisdom House, 1978.

AUDIO TAPES:
Dance for Me When I Die, CompCare, 1989.
Life Is Goodbye/Life Is Hello, CompCare, 1989.

Julia Barkley

Julia Barkley, the mother of five children and a business woman, began painting as a returning college student. She took a studio art class to fill the requirements for an Interior Design degree. Before long, however, she realized that in painting she had found her voice, her way of expressing and clarifying her ideas and beliefs.

She paints energy, life force, her love of beauty and the land. Her themes include beauty, equality, peace, and ecology. She says "to understand both the size and the content of my work, one must remember the dramatic color, the open land, and the large skies of South Dakota," her birthplace. She has studied astronomy, theology, women's spirituality, and Native American traditions.

ONE-WOMAN EXHIBITIONS:
Ward-Nasse Gallery, New York, New York, 1977, '79, '80, '82, '84, '88, '90.
University of South Dakota, 1990.
St. Mark's Lutheran Church, Minneapolis, Minnesota, 1989-1990.
Center in the City, Minneapolis, Minnesota, 1989, 1990.
Cathedral Church of St. Mark, Minneapolis, Minnesota, 1975, 1977, 1980, 1990.
Mankato State University, Mankato, Minnesota, 1982, 1988.
Ten Year Retrospective, WCAA, Buffalo, Minnesota, 1984.
WARM Gallery, Minneapolis, Minnesota, 1977, 1978, 1979, 1981.
Hennepin Methodist Church, Minneapolis, Minnesota, 1979.
Plymouth Congregational Church, Minneapolis, Minnesota, 1978.
Woodale Lutheran Church, Minneapolis, Minnesota, 1977-78.
Ingrish Gallery, Chicago, Illinois, 1977.
College of St. Catherine, St. Paul, Minnesota, 1977.
West Bank Art Gallery, Minneapolis, Minnesota, 1974, 1975.

INTERNATIONAL EXHIBITIONS:
Tokyo Fine Arts Museum, Veno Park, Tokyo, Japan, May 1980.
Hiroshima Peace Memorial Garden Hall, Hiroshima City, Japan, May 1980.

BOOK ILLUSTRATIONS:
In the Name of the Bee & the Bear & the Butterfly, by Alla Bozarth-Campbell.

GROUP EXHIBITIONS:
Women's Art Registry of Minnesota (WARM) Gallery, Minneapolis, Minnesota, 1977, 1989.
Art Expo, New York, 1983.
Lutheran Brotherhood, Minneapolis, Minnesota, 1983.
Madison Square Garden Show, 1982.
Artist's Choice: Women in the Arts Show, New York, New York, 1976.
WARM Gallery Members' Opening, Minneapolis, Minnesota, 1976.
International Women's Festival Slide Show Exhibition, 1976.
Ward-Nasse Gallery All-Member Salon Show, New York, New York, 1976.
International Women's Art Festival, Women's Interart Center, New York, New York, 1976.
WARM, Normandale Community College, Bloomington, Minnesota, "Woman-art," 1975.
Northern States Power Show, Minneapolis, Minnesota, 1975.

Terri Berthiaume Hawthorne

Terri Berthiaume Hawthorne is the eldest of seven children in a large extended family. Her parents and grandparents instilled in her the valuing of children, family ties and a love of learning. Her paternal grandmother, Winne, a central figure in a large second generation immigrant family, taught Terri about loving, nurturing and caring for many people in small ways. Her maternal grandmother, Inger, immigrated to the United States from Denmark as a young bride with an infant daughter. She taught her family the courage of listening to one's self and one's body, to work hard, to take risks, to make hard choices, and to let go when it is necessary.

Terri has been married for twenty-eight years in an evolving, caring and mutually respectful relationship. She is the mother of four adult sons and has two daughters-in-law and two grandchildren. As she moves into her "grandmothering" or crone years, she looks forward to having time to transform her mothering, nurturing skills to a societal and global level.

As a feminist and member of the 12-Step Community (AA, Alanon, Alateen, etc.), she values the telling of and listening to stories. She says, "By providing community to one another we are learning to say what has been unsayable, to know what we have been afraid to know, to reach new levels of honesty and to take some of the risks needed to formulate new ways of living and loving." She practices women's spirituality or eco-feminism. With her family, she is an active member of a Unitarian Universalist church.

Terri is an educator, counselor, ritualist, author, photographer, publisher, and producer. She has twenty years experience working with women, men and children in the areas of spirituality, art, counseling and chemical abuse recovery and prevention. Based on her interest in eco-feminist spirituality, quantum physics, new science philosophies, and new models of leadership, she organizes and develops programs, materials, exercises, media presentations, and rituals on these topics. She prefers to work in multi media formats, where she weaves together ideas, art work and poetry from many sources.

She holds a Bachelor of Arts degree in Psychology and Women's Studies and a Master of Science degree in Women Studies.

BOOKS:
The Goddess in the Age of Quantum Physics, 1988, Tara Education Publications, St. Paul, Minnesota.
The Many Faces of the Great Mother, 1987, in partnership with Diane Brown, Tara Education Publications, St. Paul, Minnesota.
Children Are People Support Group Manual, 1985, Children Are People, St. Paul, Minnesota.

ARTICLES:
"Art and Ritual," *The Spiral Path: Essays and Interviews on Women's Spirituality, Edition II,* 1990, Ed. Theresa King O'Brien, Yes Publications, St. Paul, Minnesota.
"Cultural and Historical Aspects of Mythology," *The Language of Myth: An Introduction to the Ideas of Joseph Campbell,* 1989, Rev. Ted Tollefson, St. Paul, Minnesota.

SLIDE PRESENTATIONS:
Terri has produced many slide presentations and is currently working on a video series entitled, *A Woman's Perspective on Mythology or The Goddess in the Age of Quantum Physics.*